Not by Bread Alone

Daily Reflections for Lent 2011

Bishop Robert F. Morneau

LITURGICAL PRESS

Collegeville, Minnesota

www.litpress.org

Nihil Obstat: Rev. Robert C. Harren, J.C.L.
Imprimatur: ✠ Most Rev. John F. Kinney, J.C.D., D.D., Bishop of St. Cloud, Minnesota, January 29, 2010.

Cover design by Ann Blattner. Photograph courtesy of Photos.com.

ISSN: 1550-803X

ISBN: 978-0-8146-3309-0

Introduction

Baron Friedrich von Hugel (1852–1925), an influential spiritual writer and director, had the practice of spending fifteen minutes a day doing devotional reading. He did this for over forty years, reading slowly and prayerfully books such as the Bible, the *Confessions of St. Augustine*, *The Imitation of Christ*, and many more. The analogy he used for this devotional reading, in contrast to "ordinary" reading, was like "letting a very slowly dissolving lozenge melt imperceptibly in your mouth."

During this season of Lent we do well to let this "best practice" nourish our soul by this type of devotional reading, one that engages the soul, elevates our spiritual horizons, and empowers us to taste the presence of God in a new way. No hurry; no attempt to cover ground; no seeking large quantities of information. This type of reading leads to transformation and a new quality of life. Devotional (spiritual) reading leads to intimacy with the Lord and growth in taking on the concerns of God.

This volume sets forth scriptural passages and biblical reflections that are aimed at this unique type of reading. In less than five hundred words a day one is invited to let these verbal lozenges slowly dissolve in one's mind and heart. By taking ten to fifteen minutes a day in meditative prayer we will be well prepared for the Easter mysteries.

Beware! If this spiritual reading is genuine, be assured that the Lord will ask you to take his word and translate it into action. This assurance is grounded in the Ash Wednesday imperatives that we are to pray, fast, and give alms. The giving of alms is more than monetary contributions. It involves reaching out to the needy in a variety of ways. Just as we might commit ourselves to fifteen minutes a day of devotional reading, we might also commit ourselves to a specific concern this Lent, such as feeding the poor, visiting the sick, instructing the ignorant, or some other corporal or spiritual work of mercy.

All of this is part of our discipleship. Following Jesus entails a lived baptismal commitment. Like Jesus, we are to be agents of God's light, love, and life. It is no wonder that so many people have found the prayer of St. Francis to be so meaningful since it is a request that we become true instruments of God's peace, joy, hope, and love. In that prayer we are reminded time and time again that it is precisely in dying, like Jesus, that we are born to eternal life.

We begin with the end in mind: Easter! All of Lent is a preparation to celebrate the Easter mysteries. It is by participating in Jesus' life, suffering, and death that we are given a share in his resurrection. Lent is all about new life, a new life that comes only when the grain of wheat dies unto itself and is born anew.

Reflections

March 9: Ash Wednesday

Divine Compensation

Readings: Joel 2:12-18; 2 Cor 5:20–6:2; Matt 6:1-6, 16-18

Scripture:
Jesus said to his disciples:
    "Take care not to perform righteous deeds
    in order that people may see them;
    otherwise, you will have no recompense from your
        heavenly Father." (Matt 6:1)

Reflection: Many people employed by major institutions are given compensation packages, perks, if you will. Along with their base salary, there might be such items as health insurance, travel expenses, housing allowance, and so forth. In some instances, these perks amount to over 30 percent of one's total contract.

In "working" for the Lord, disciples are promised a reward, the gift of eternal life. Now *there* is a compensation package. But there are strings attached. One of them is that we do the right things for the right reasons, that is, that we do righteous deeds with the proper motivation.

Jesus advises us not to go around blowing a trumpet as we do the righteous deed of helping the poor. Jesus advises us not to run up into the sanctuary or kneel down at street corners when we pray. Such attention seeking is not appropriate. And, when we do our deeds of mortification—those acts of self-denial that help us to become interiorly free—Jesus advises us against putting on a sad face.

What should our motivation be in giving alms, praying, and fasting? Is it that we receive public recognition or even eternal life? It would seem not. We do these righteous deeds because they have intrinsic value. In and of themselves, they promote life and are building blocks for the kingdom of God. As we serve others, God is glorified; as we contemplate and give thanks, God is glorified; when we discipline our appetites and order our energies toward fullness of life, God is glorified.

St. Ignatius of Loyola, founder of the Society of Jesus, gave his community a powerful motto: *Ad majorem Dei gloriam* ("For the greater glory of God"). Here is the proper motivation for the Christian life. The same message is given in the Divine Office where we read: "Let mind and heart be in your song: this is to glorify God with your whole self" (Hesychius).

Meditation: What are your resolutions for this Lent? What do you understand by divine compensation?

Prayer: Lord Jesus, may this season of Lent be truly holy. May we glorify the Father by our prayer, fasting, and almsgiving. Purify our motivation; give us the gift of your Holy Spirit so that all we think, feel, and do may bring your kingdom into fuller realization.

The Rest of the Story

Readings: Deut 30:15-20; Luke 9:22-25

Scripture:
Jesus said to his disciples:
"The Son of Man must suffer greatly and be rejected
by the elders, the chief priests, and the scribes,
and be killed and on the third day be raised."
(Luke 9:22)

Reflection: On this second day of Lent, we are already given the rest of the story. Lent is about the paschal mystery and our preparation for the great Easter mysteries. Lent is about the life, suffering, death, and resurrection of Jesus. Because we know the end, we can prepare well to participate in this mystery of our faith by saying yes to the cross we are given to carry and know that by losing our life, like Jesus, we might gain it.

When all is said and done, everything comes back to the options that Moses presents: life or death, prosperity or doom, blessing or curse. What is at issue is human freedom: will we, individually and collectively, obey God's decrees, or will we go our separate ways, turning our hearts away from God and not listening and responding to his commands? Here is the true fundamental option: to obey or not to obey. On our choice rests our destiny, indeed, the destiny of the world.

At the very beginning of his encyclical letter *Spe Salvi* (On Christian Hope), Pope Benedict XVI comments that "hope enables us to face the present assured that it leads to a goal worthy of our efforts." In following Jesus, the Master, who suffered, was rejected, and was killed, the disciples had to have hope, hope in the mystery of the resurrection and eternal life. Jesus assured them of that, and it was hope and faith that sustained them in their embrace of the cross.

Our responsorial psalm gives us a mantra for the day: "Blessed are they who hope in the Lord" (Ps 40:5a). Here is the hope of the tree planted near the river of life; here is the hope of sinners who look upon the face of Christ; here is the hope that is grounded in faith and expresses itself in love.

Meditation: Looking back over the past five years, what religious practices helped you most in preparing for Easter? What is your level of hope? Indeed, of faith and love?

Prayer: Jesus, you invite us into the life of discipleship. In doing so you lay out the conditions involved in following you: participation in your suffering, a willingness to die for others, a life of sacrificial self-giving. It is only through the gift of the Holy Spirit that we can remain faithful and do the Father's will with joy.

Forms of Fasting

Readings: Isa 58:1-9a; Matt 9:14-15

Scripture:
Jesus answered them, "Can the wedding guests mourn
   as long as the bridegroom is with them?
The days will come when the bridegroom is taken from
      them,
   and then they will fast." (Matt 9:15)

Reflection: Common sense tells us that on joyful occasions
we celebrate; common sense tells us that in times of tragedy
and loss we mourn. So when it comes to a wedding or a
significant anniversary or some major achievement, we pull
out all the stops and rejoice. When death comes or some form
of illness or major loss crosses our path, we grieve and la-
ment. Such is the manner in which we deal with the joys and
sorrows of life.

Two days ago, on Ash Wednesday, we were given the imperative to fast. Just as there is a time for everything—a time
to be born and a time to die—so too is there a time to fast and
a time to refrain from fasting. It is inappropriate to fast at a
wedding banquet. To do so would simply make one a killjoy.
But in times of suffering and loss, or in seasons of discipline,
fasting is not only appropriate but also necessary.

Isaiah the prophet shares with us the forms of fasting that God wants: "Setting free the oppressed, / breaking every yoke; / Sharing your bread with the hungry, / sheltering the oppressed and the homeless; / Clothing the naked when you see them, / and not turning your back on your own" (Isa 58:6b-7). Fasting is for the sake of life, not death; fasting is about liberation, not incarceration. While on the one hand fasting can involve mortifying ourselves by less amounts of food or keeping night vigils, a deeper form of fasting leads to a fuller life for oneself and others.

Our gospel verse reads: "Seek good and not evil so that you may live, / and the LORD will be with you." Jesus is the bridegroom; Jesus is always with us. Our fasting in his presence is not a form of mourning. Rather, our discipline of seeking good and refraining from evil is our attempt to be disposed to recognize the Lord's presence, a presence often manifest in the oppressed, the poor, and the hurting. The call here is to be better agents of God's life and love.

Meditation: What kind of fasting is meaningful to you? What specific form of fasting is the Lord asking of you this Lent?

Prayer: Jesus, our bridegroom, you continue to invite us to your table. As we rejoice in your presence, help us to be conscious of all those who live on the margins of society. May our fasting draw them more closely into your presence and into your love.

The Divine Physician

Readings: Isa 58:9b-14; Luke 5:27-32

Scripture:
Jesus said to them in reply,
   "Those who are healthy do not need a physician, but the
      sick do.
I have not come to call the righteous to repentance but sin-
      ners." (Luke 5:31-32)

Reflection: William James, the noted American philosopher
and psychologist, gave the Gifford Lectures at Edinburgh
between 1901 and 1902. His lectures were published in *The
Varieties of Religious Experience: A Study of Human Nature*. In
lectures 6 and 7, James spoke of "The Sick Soul" and listed
various characteristics that lead to sickness and melancholy:
loathing, irritation, exasperation, self-mistrust, self-despair,
suspicion, anxiety, trepidation, fear. Such elements lead to a
morbid-minded person.

   By contrast, "we give the name of healthy-mindedness to
the tendency which looks on all things and sees that they are
good." As the divine physician, Jesus came to give us health
and fullness of life. We are called to put on the mind and
heart of the Lord, seeing that creation is good in its deepest
recesses. Jesus also calls us to face our dark side, our melancholy and sickness, indeed, our sins. Christianity is not about

romanticism, obscuring the presence of evil. Christianity deals with brutal realism, rubbing our noses into the truth of things.

Levi heard the invitation to health: "Follow me." Inviting Jesus to eat and drink with him and his fellow tax collectors, Levi ventured more deeply into the life of Jesus. Despite the complaint of the Pharisees and scribes, Levi, like Zacchaeus, held his ground and became the host of his savior, the one who called him to righteousness. One can only wonder how many other tax collectors and guests were changed by that fateful dinner.

In "leaving everything," we can well imagine that Levi's repentance involved not only conversion of his conduct but also a change in his thought patterns and values. Having experienced God's gratuitous love, Levi now stood eternally indebted to the one who stopped at the customs post and said: "Follow me."

Meditation: How has Jesus been a physician in your life? What are the elements of repentance that you will be working on this Lent?

Prayer: Lord Jesus, you came to cure the sick; you came to cure us sinners. May we have no fear in inviting you to eat and drink at our table. May we hear daily your call to follow you. Give us the grace of repentance. Make us whole in your grace.

Temptations Abound

Readings: Gen 2:7-9; 3:1-7; Rom 5:12-19 or 5:12, 17-19; Matt 4:1-11

Scripture:
At that time Jesus was led by the Spirit into the desert
   to be tempted by the devil.
He fasted forty days and forty nights,
   and afterwards he was hungry. (Matt 4:1-2)

Reflection: There are two pieces of geography that smell of solitude: deserts and mountains. Away from the madding crowd, we travelers bump up against the rawness of reality. Distractions are gone and we come face-to-face with the mysteries of life, a complex life of good and evil.

Jesus faced three temptations in the desert: the temptation to live on bread alone, the temptation to test God's providence, and the temptation to idolatry. Jesus remained obedient and thwarted each temptation by turning to the word of God. It was the Father's will that dominated his mission and kept him faithful.

Adam and Eve were not in a desert but in the lushness of a primordial garden. They too faced temptations and we know the rest of the story: the fruit was eaten, their eyes were opened, and they landed east of Eden. Like Jesus, they were faced with choices; unlike Jesus, they refused obedience and found themselves separated from one another and their Creator.

St. Paul experienced both disobedience and obedience. This great disciple to the Gentiles lived to write about the horrendous nature of sin and the abundance of God's grace. Always his focus was on Jesus, the obedient one. It was in Christ that God's gracious gift of righteousness was to be found. We can feel in Paul's writings someone who knew both the agony of Adam's sin and the beauty and joy of Jesus' faithful ministry.

We are all called to spend time in the desert, up on the mountain, and in God's vast garden we call creation. In all of those geographies, we will face decisions. In all of those places we will face temptations. Our need is for angels to come and minister to us lest we, like Adam and Eve, lose our focus. Like Paul, we know, deep down, that we can do all things in Christ who strengthens us (Phil 4:13).

Meditation: What are the geographies of your life? What are the places where you were tempted to do good or evil? What have been your experiences of sin and grace?

Prayer: Lord Jesus, as we venture more deeply into this Lenten season, send your Spirit into our hearts that we might remain faithful to your word and your way. So many temptations pull at us; so many distractions prevent us from living in your presence. In your kindness, send angels to minister to us.

Lest We Forget: Eschatology

Readings: Lev 19:1-2, 11-18; Matt 25:31-46

Scripture:
"When the Son of Man comes in his glory,
and all the angels with him,
he will sit upon his glorious throne,
and all the nations will be assembled before him."
    (Matt 25:31-32a)

Reflections: Eschatology is that branch of theology that studies the "last things"—death, particular judgment, heaven, hell, purgatory, the Lord's second coming, the kingdom of God. But the ultimate eschaton, the ultimate last thing, is God. To study eschatology is to be involved in reflecting on our very destiny, our life with God.

Eschatology has fallen on hard times. The tyranny of the immediate moment distracts us from pondering the larger questions that reside deep in the soul, those questions of our identity and our destiny. Yet these questions cannot be totally silenced. At wake services and funerals, at times of national disasters (e.g., 9/11) and warfare, the question of the end time keeps surfacing. What is life all about? Where are we going?

Such is the case in today's gospel. Anyone who seriously ponders Matthew 25:31-46 is caught up in questions of eschatology. At the end, we all stand before the judgment seat of God. At the end time, there are but two options: eternal punishment or eternal life. And the determining factor in this scriptural passage is our treatment of others. The Son of Man separates the sheep from the goats by the standard of active concern or negligence for our sisters and brothers.

The council fathers of the Second Vatican Council (1962–65) were concerned about eschatology. In the council's great document, *Lumen Gentium* (Dogmatic Constitution on the Church), we find chapter 7 titled "The Eschatological Nature of the Pilgrim Church and Her Union with the Heavenly Church." Again, the teaching church reminds us that we are bound for the glory of heaven and to be with all the saints in eternal life.

We are dealing here with a Christian perspective, a Christian worldview. Obviously, many do not agree, and, from a naturalistic point of view, death has finality. We are born, we grow, we diminish, we die. There is nothing beyond the grave. The eschatological question is foolishness. Not so for Jesus. This life takes on meaning because there is such a thing as eternal life, our life with God and all those who do God's will.

Meditation: How much thought do you give to the question of eternity? What does Matthew's last judgment scene say to your heart?

Prayer: Gracious and loving God, give us the gift of faith. May we see our existence as you see it; may we live our lives in a way that you desire. We are a pilgrim people and we have a positive orientation toward eternal life. Guide us home safely.

Spiritual Verbosity

Readings: Isa 55:10-11; Matt 6:7-15

Scripture:
Jesus said to his disciples:
> "In praying, do not babble like the pagans,
> who think that they will be heard because of their many
>   words.
Do not be like them." (Matt 6:7-8a)

Reflection: On our spiritual journey, we all need mentors and models. So we turn to the saints and prophets, to theologians and religious, to faith-filled people to understand the various dimensions of our life in God, especially in our need to learn about the nature and methodologies of prayer. And, of course, we turn to Jesus, who is the teacher of prayer and the one we are to emulate.

Jesus cautions us: do not babble. Verbosity does not assure a hearing before the mystery of God. Rather, we are to use simple, direct, succinct discourse. We are to address God as Father and pray from the heart. There are seven basic petitions, each of them filled with rich meaning, that Jesus recommends we make as we stand before our loving God. To pray this prayer slowly and with deep mindfulness means that we have learned well what the Lord is asking of us.

What does prayer do, we may ask? This mutual dialogue deepens our relationship with God; it fosters unity and intimacy. Prayer refines the heart and broadens the intellect. Prayer reveals our true self before the living and true God. Prayer basically does one thing: connects us to the truth, the Truth who is Jesus.

A Doctor of the Church, St. Francis de Sales (1567–1622), offers this advice: "for the best prayer is that which keeps us so occupied with God that we don't think about ourselves or about what we are doing." This great teacher encourages simplicity, gentleness, and trust in the Lord. It is obvious that St. Francis de Sales understood the teaching of Jesus and has passed on to us the fine art of praying.

What beauty there is in a friendship where even words are not necessary. Just being in the presence of the one loved is sufficient. By contrast, when verbosity reigns, when there is constant chatter and incessant speaking, one has to wonder if authentic encounter is being avoided. Jesus encourages us to call God our Father and adds but a few petitions.

Meditation: What is your method of praying? What are your favorite prayers and how did you come upon them?

Prayer: Lord Jesus, we are slow learners. Too often we complicate prayer by an overabundance of words. Send your Spirit into our hearts to teach us how to pray. Only then will we come to hear and respond to your loving presence.

Does Anything Happen?

Readings: Jonah 3:1-10; Luke 11:29-32

Scripture:
"At the judgment the men of Nineveh will arise with this
      generation
   and condemn it,
   because at the preaching of Jonah they repented,
   and there is something greater than Jonah here."
      (Luke 11:32)

Reflection: Would that we had a video of Jonah preaching in
the city of Nineveh. We are told straight out that his ministry
was most effective: the people of Nineveh (even the king and
the cattle) repented and their city was spared. In other words,
when Jonah preached, something happened. That claim cannot be made by many preachers, modern and postmodern.

Apparently, Jonah's message was relatively short: "Forty
days more and Nineveh shall be destroyed." A little fire and
brimstone discourse had its effect. Everybody fasted; they
donned sackcloth, covered themselves with ashes, and the
Lord's blazing wrath was avoided. Once there was a preacher
in New Jersey whose Easter homily consisted of four words:
"Alleluia. Jesus is risen!" That was half as many words as
Jonah's homily and one wonders how many lives were
changed by this address.

Jesus was a preacher man. He was a truth-teller. Without mincing words, he proclaimed that the generation of his times was evil, so much so that no sign would be sufficient to turn them around into the way of goodness. Even though his ministry was infinitely more powerful than that of Jonah, the people of Nineveh had enough sense to heed Jonah's eight words and reform their lives. Even Jesus' death on the cross could not convince the crowds of God's love and mercy.

William James (1842–1910), the noted American philosopher and psychologist, gave the Gifford Lectures in Scotland between 1901 and 1902. In lecture 4, dealing with "The Religion of Healthy-Mindedness," James writes: "We have now whole congregations whose preachers, far from magnifying our consciousness of sin, seem devoted rather to making little of it." Preachers have a balancing act: indeed, they are called to name our demons and sins; they are also called to make manifest the workings of God's love and mercy. Jonah and Jesus were involved in that task. While not minimizing the reality of sin, the ultimate message was one of good news: our salvation through the graciousness of God.

Meditation: In what ways has preaching enriched or diminished your spiritual life? What was the best homily/sermon that you ever heard? Why?

Prayer: Come, Holy Spirit, come. Enlighten all of us to hear and understand your word. Bless all preachers; bless all congregations. Fill us with the message of truth and wisdom, and guide us in the way of your eternal love and mercy.

Ask, Seek, Knock!!!

Readings: Esth C:12, 14-16, 23-25; Matt 7:7-12

Scripture:
Jesus said to his disciples:
"Ask and it will be given to you;
seek and you will find;
knock and the door will be opened to you." (Matt 7:7)

Reflection: In 1942, Warner Sallman painted the scene of Jesus knocking at the door, a door that had no outside handle. If the door were to be opened, it had to be opened from the inside. The painting was a rendition of Revelation 3:20, a verse in which the Lord is seeking entrance into our lives. A great Lenten question: will we allow Jesus to come into our souls and dine with us?

When Jesus tells the disciples to ask, to seek, and to knock, we must realize that Jesus is always the one to take the initiative. He first knocks at the door of our life before we knock on the door of heaven; he seeks out the lost sheep long before the flock seeks the Good Shepherd; he asks us to share our gifts with others before we ask him for renewed grace. Again, we are to emulate the God in whose image and likeness we are made.

So, what will you ask for this Lent? Better health? A deeper prayer life? The healing of relationships? Greater wisdom and compassion? The gift of tears, tears of repentance? A world of justice and peace? These are noble requests. Yet, too often we ask for greater personal recognition, more possessions or control, an increase in comfort and security. We are co-opted by our culture and it is only through the grace of the Holy Spirit that we request what is best for others and for ourselves.

So, what do you seek? The widow sought her lost coin; the shepherd, his lost sheep; the father, his prodigal son. We are all searchers and everyone seeks some form of meaning to life. Most people seek integration in a broken world. Many are looking for depth in a world of superficiality. Such goals are noble. Yet, we can also chase after rainbows and waste our time looking for that nonexistent pot of gold.

So, where do you go to find the Lord? In what sacred geography does God dwell? All we have to do is turn toward the mystery of creation and there, in the starry, starry night, in the flight of the eagle, in the beauty of the ocean and mountain, we are immersed in the "divine milieu." And we can be assured that if we knock, the Lord will open.

Meditation: What does your heart seek? In what ways does God take the initiative in your life? Have you opened the door to our "pilgrim" God?

Prayer: Come, Holy Spirit, teach us your ways. Give us the wisdom to ask and to seek and to knock in all the proper places. Prevent us from wasting our time and energy on things that do not matter. Instruct us in your ways, the ways of love, peace, and joy.

March 18: Friday of the First Week of Lent

Bad Blood

Readings: Ezek 18:21-28; Matt 5:20-26

Scripture:
"Therefore, if you bring your gift to the altar,
   and there recall that your brother
   has anything against you,
   leave your gift there at the altar,
   go first and be reconciled with your brother,
   and then come and offer your gift." (Matt 5:23-24)

Reflection: The expression "bad blood" refers to a disposition of vindictiveness or ill-feeling. Within our family systems and communities, feuds can exist for years, even decades. We see this on the international level as we watch what is happening in the Middle East, in southeast Asia, in the cold and hot wars that crisscross our planet. But we need not look that far for bad blood: it exists sometimes in our own hearts.

The kingdom of God is about union and unity: union with God and unity with one another. Sin breaks that unity; feuds and bad blood injure the union that God desires for all his children. Thus, we are in a constant state of reconciliation, attempting to mend broken relationships, asking forgiveness for our sins, seeking peace with those who have hurt us or those whom we have injured. St. Paul constantly reminds the early Christians that they have been entrusted with the ministry of reconciliation.

As we come to the altar to hear God's word and receive the Eucharist, we are challenged to examine our conscience to see if reconciliation is needed. Jesus is clear and emphatic: if someone has something against us, we are to seek unity in that relationship before we celebrate it at the altar.

Sometimes that is impossible. The person we are in conflict with may have died. Or, there is no openness on the part of the other for healing. All that can be done is to make a sincere effort, and then we leave the rest to God. Even Jesus at the Last Supper and on the cross had to deal with bad blood as Judas betrayed him. The lack of union and unity was as painful as the physical torture.

John Macquarrie, the Anglican theologian, writes: "By 'reconciliation' is meant the activity whereby the disorders of existence are healed, its imbalance redressed, its alienation bridged over." He might have added: "When bad blood dries up."

Meditation: How can you be a minister of reconciliation this Lent? Is there any bad blood in your relationships?

Prayer: Lord Jesus, as we come to the altar give us the grace to deal with the disorders in our relationships. Remove the bad blood from our communities and world. Then we shall worship you in spirit and in truth.

Dreams: Part of Life's Stuff

Readings: 2 Sam 7:4-5a, 12-14a, 16; Rom 4:13, 16-18, 22; Matt 1:16, 18-21, 24a or Luke 2:41-51a

Scripture:
"Joseph, son of David,
   do not be afraid to take Mary your wife into your home.
For it was through the Holy Spirit
   that this child has been conceived in her." (Matt 1:20b)

Reflection: Not all dreams are to be trusted. Some are just weird, strange, eccentric, and we know not whence they came. But the dream of Joseph proved to be true. First of all, he was afraid and the angel named the emotion. Right there is found some justification that this dream is for real. Second, Joseph was given inside information as to Mary's conception. The acceptance of this piece of news demanded faith and trust. Joseph, being a righteous man, embraced the message and did what God had commanded.

It is one thing to hear a message, be it from a dream, a passage of Scripture, some insight from a wisdom figure, and it is another thing to be obedient to what is asked. Time and time again we see the biblical characters Abraham, Jeremiah, Mary herself—being approached with a mission that appears so overwhelming as to cause trepidation. Indeed, they protest that what is being asked cannot be fulfilled. And yet, graced with obedient faith, they do the bidding of the Lord.

One of the constant refrains in the writings of Douglas V. Steere, a Quaker, is that we are called to a life of "attention, adherence, and abandonment to God's undivided sway." Joseph was mindful of what God asked of him; Joseph, despite initial hesitation, adhered to what God desired; Joseph, in that marvel of obedient faith, gave his life over to the divine design. This attention, adherence, and abandonment is the vocation of all people, regardless of one's unique call.

Prospero, in Shakespeare's *The Tempest*, is no angel but he did have a message: "We are such stuff / As dreams are made of, and our little life / Is rounded with a sleep." Joseph's "little life" had big consequences. He participated in the mystery of redemption in a unique way by being Mary's husband and Jesus' stepfather. Joseph came through the tempest of a midnight dream and helped change the world.

Meditation: Has God ever spoken to you in a dream? Do you see your vocation like that of Joseph—a life of obedient faith?

Prayer: St. Joseph, intercede for us. Help us to be attentive to God's call, be it in a dream or in our waking hours. May we play our role in the mystery of redemption. May our little lives bear rich consequences.

Mountains and Valleys

Readings: Gen 12:1-4a; 2 Tim 1:8b-10; Matt 17:1-9

Scripture:
Then Peter said to Jesus in reply,
  "Lord, it is good that we are here.
If you wish, I will make three tents here,
  one for you, one for Moses, and one for Elijah."
    (Matt 17:4)

Reflection: The camera industry has flourished because we humans long to hang on to experiences of beauty and goodness. So we fill our albums with photos from baptisms and weddings, picnics and anniversaries, mountains and sunsets, stars and rainbows. Since Peter forgot his camera, he thought that by building three shelters, the experience of the transfigured Jesus might be sustained. After all, how could Moses and Elijah leave when such thoughtful hospitality was being offered?

Human life is transitory. Things come and go in successive fashion and we are forever trying to hang on to the patches of beauty and goodness that come our way. These mountain-top experiences are special and powerful graces. Yet, down the mountain we go since our life in the valley has its own significance. The challenge for Peter, James, and John (and us as well) is to have the vision of faith to see Jesus manifest as much in the valley as on the mountaintop.

Brother Edward Seifert, a member of the Christian Brothers, wrote a poem titled "On the Ridge." In it, the poet raises the question of what it would be like to live up high on a ridge, overlooking the beauty of autumn forests, a winding river, rolling hills. Although this geography offers its special blessing—as does listening to a symphony or having morning tea—we cannot make this "place" a permanent residence. No, down into the valley we must go while not forgetting the "sudden look of creation" that we received.

The transfiguration is about contemplation and action. Our lives are about those gracious moments of loving attention to God's truth, goodness, and beauty, as well as the summons to serve and to encounter Jesus in the community of humankind. One can feel the tension inside Peter as he longed to remain atop the mountain and yet wanted to do what Jesus asked of him.

Meditation: What have been some of your mountaintop experiences? How do you deal with the transitoriness of life? Describe the valley God has called you to.

Prayer: Jesus, you manifested yourself to Peter, James, and John on the mountain. You manifest yourself to us in Scripture and sacraments, in community and the movements of our hearts. Help us to see your glory; help us to serve you in our needy sisters and brothers.

Rembrandt, Jessica Powers, and Shakespeare

Readings: Dan 9:4b-10; Luke 6:36-38

Scripture:
Jesus said to his disciples:
"Be merciful, just as your Father is merciful." (Luke 6:36)

Reflection: Rembrandt Harmanszoon Van Rijn (1606–69) was extremely prodigious, leaving the world some six hundred paintings, three hundred etchings, and sixteen hundred drawings. One of his classic works is his painting of the return of the prodigal son. This painting, for many individuals, captures the essence of God's mercy. We would do well during this season of Lent to spend several hours contemplating this portrait while reading the biblical account in Luke 15:11-32.

While we witness the father's mercy, there are other things happening in the background of the painting, such things as judgment and condemnation. It would appear that justice is bypassed. After all, the elder son remained home and was faithful to his duties while the younger son wasted his inheritance, sinned, and showed great disrespect for his father. Yet the father forgives. More, a banquet is held and more gifts are given: a robe, a ring, and a father's affection.

In our first reading from Daniel we hear that God preserves the "merciful covenant." What grace this is for us who have sinned. Though we have turned away from God's love, God remains faithful and continually invites us back into his embrace. The Ash Wednesday refrain echoes in our hearts: "Turn away from sin and be faithful to the Gospel." Turn away from sin and experience once again a God who is rich in mercy.

The Carmelite poet Jessica Powers (Sister Miriam of the Holy Spirit, her religious name) wrote about God as being clothed in robes of mercy. In her poem "The Garments of God," we hear that God dwells in the darkness of our souls and our great prayer is not that of words but of clinging to God's voluminous garments of mercy. What good theology here; what consoling wisdom.

If Rembrandt paints mercy for us, Shakespeare wraps words around this quality. In *The Merchant of Venice* we read: "We do pray for mercy, / and that same prayer doth teach us all to render / The deeds of mercy." Shakespeare proves here to be a good spiritual director.

Meditation: From whom have you received mercy and forgiveness? To whom have you offered these graces? Why is judging and condemning so dangerous to the soul?

Prayer: Merciful Father, we are made in your image and likeness. Through the power of your Spirit help us to be ministers of your mercy and love. Too easily we judge, condemn, and fail to forgive. Heal us. Strengthen us in your ways.

The Seduction of Recognition

Readings: Isa 1:10, 16-20; Matt 23:1-12

Scripture:
"They [scribes and Pharisees] love places of honor at banquets, seats of honor in synagogues,
  greetings in marketplaces, and the salutation 'Rabbi.'"
   (Matt 23:6-7)

Reflection: Who doesn't like to be acknowledged in public? Yet, how seductive it is to seek prestige and acclaim. It may, even for a time, bring some level of satisfaction, perhaps a modicum of happiness. But, in the end, it is a dead-end street just as is the vast accumulation of possessions and a life centered on pleasure. Life is not about exaltation of one's ego; life is about seeking and sharing truth and love.

Jesus preaches humility, that virtue that is the gateway into truth. And the truth is that, indeed, we have but one Father; the truth is that greatness is found in service and self-sacrifice. People who live in the truth, that is, people who are humble, realize that all is gift and that we are here on earth to be recipients and transmitters of God's grace.

Blessed Mother Teresa of Calcutta (1910–97) abhorred public recognition and urged the sisters in her community, Missionaries of Charity, to embrace poverty and shun any worldly acclaim. Mother Teresa wrote: "By Absolute Poverty

I mean real and complete poverty—not starving—but wanting—just only what the real poor have—to be really dead to all that the world claims for its own." No places of honor, no seats of honor, no sought-after greetings and salutation for Mother Teresa. She simply wanted to go on her humble way serving the poorest of the poor. No wonder she is great in the eyes of God.

Mother Teresa heard the Lord's word; Mother Teresa listened to God's instruction to come and be his light. She made justice her aim, as Isaiah urges; she defended the widow and reached out to the orphans. This "saint of Calcutta" preached by example and demonstrated to the world what true greatness is all about and what humility means.

Meditation: Who are the great people in your life? What qualities do they have? Why is recognition so seductive? Why is humility so difficult?

Prayer: Jesus, you invite us, as you did Mother Teresa, to come and be your light. Give us the courage to be instruments of your grace and teach us the ways of sacrificial love. May we emulate you in washing others' feet and serve those who are in need. Come, Lord Jesus, come.

The Eucharistic Secret

Readings: Jer 18:18-20; Matt 20:17-28

Scripture:
Jesus said in reply,
  "You do not know what you are asking.
Can you drink the chalice that I am going to drink?"
They said to him, "We can." (Matt 20:22)

Reflection: Evelyn Underhill (1875–1941), one of the finest spiritual writers of the twentieth century, spoke of the eucharistic secret as having two halves: the breaking of bread and the sharing of the cup of Jesus' passion. Unless both halves come together something essential is missing in our life of discipleship.

This insight should put to rest the false dichotomy of whether the Eucharist is meal or sacrifice, table or altar, primarily bread or wine. Jesus invites us to both break and share word and bread with him, as well as drink of the same self-giving sacrifice. Jesus calls us to the table of friendship and conversation as well as to the altar of total self-donation. Jesus feeds us with the bread of life and the wine of salvation. Only when both the breaking of bread and the sharing in the cup are understood and lived do we come close to comprehending some dimension of the eucharistic secret.

The mother of James and John had an ambitious desire: that her sons would have prominent positions in God's kingdom. A laudable request, indeed. But Jesus quickly informs those sons of Zebedee of two things: that a sharing in God's kingdom is contingent upon their embracing the paschal mystery (Jesus' passion, death, and resurrection) and that his Father alone determines our place in the kingdom. With notable audacity, James and John claim that they are able to drink of the cup and, as we now know, they did.

Jeremiah too had to learn of the secrets of God's design. It always comes back to dying and rising. The citizens of Jerusalem and the people of Judah would see to it that the prophet Jeremiah would suffer. The Lord himself would see to it that the prayer of Jeremiah—the prayer reminding God of his past kindness—would not go unheeded. Jeremiah lived the eucharistic secret centuries before the secret took on flesh.

Meditation: Do you see the Eucharist more as meal or sacrifice, table or altar? What cup of passion has the Lord given to you and your family? How well have you drunk of it?

Prayer: Lord Jesus, teach us the secrets of your heart. Help us to pray like Jeremiah, with honesty and courage. Help us to emulate James and John in following you to and through the cross. Make us into a eucharistic people, committed to doing your will and furthering your kingdom.

A Great Chasm

Readings: Jer 17:5-10; Luke 16:19-31

Scripture:
"Moreover, between us and you a great chasm is established
  to prevent anyone from crossing
  who might wish to go from our side to yours
  or from your side to ours." (Luke 16:26)

Reflection: Distance is not just a matter of feet, yards, or miles. Distance also applies to the vast gap between good and evil, truth and falsity, beauty and ugliness. So great is the separation here that there is no passing over from one to the other.

Jesus is again telling stories. Here we have the anonymous rich man and poor Lazarus. In death, as in life, they are separated geographically and spiritually. While living the rich man has his wealth, wardrobe, and comfort; old Lazarus has *nada*, and even his health fails him. And we know the rest of the story: Lazarus winds up in the bosom of Abraham, whereas the uncaring rich man is in torment and despair. Even though a request is made to send someone to warn the rich man's brothers, Abraham states that enough warnings have been given through the Mosaic law and the mighty prophets.

And what is the message of the prophets? For a starter we can turn to Jeremiah. He reminds us of the consequences of our actions because it is the Lord himself who probes our mind and tests our heart. God challenges us to think of the needs of others and their well-being; more, God calls us to have compassionate hearts so that we reach out to the poor and the hurting. This outward thinking and deep fellow-feeling flow out from our being near the living waters of God's grace. If our soul, like a tree, is planted near the living water of divine grace, we will bear fruit, fruit that will last.

There is a certain urgency about the Lenten season. We keep hearing that "now is the acceptable time, now is the day of salvation." Taking this to heart, each of us might ask what are the chasms and gaps in our lives. Is there a gap between hearing the word of God and actually living it? Is there a considerable distance (a light year, for example) between our mind (our thinking) and our heart (our feeling) and our behavior (deeds of commission or omission)?

Meditation: What role do the prophets and the law of Moses play in your life? What have been some moments of repentance on your faith journey and what brought them about?

Prayer: Loving God, help us to listen attentively to your word and to the presence of the One who was raised from the dead, Christ Jesus. We have gaps in our lives between your will and our own. It is only through your grace and mercy that we can bridge the "ought" and the "is." Grant us the grace of repentance through the gift of your Holy Spirit.

Elizabeth Ministry

Readings: Isa 7:10-14, 8:10; Heb 10:4-10; Luke 1:26-38

Scripture:
"And behold, Elizabeth, your relative,
  has also conceived a son in her old age,
  and this is the sixth month for her who was called barren;
  for nothing will be impossible for God." (Luke 1:36-37)

Reflection: A fairly new ministry in the church is called Elizabeth Ministry. There are seven hundred chapters internationally. The mission of this organization is to help and support women during their childbearing years. That support is extended as well to the entire family and the community. Elizabeth Ministry deals with such issues as fertility, pregnancy, adoption, infertility, post-abortion healing, miscarriage, and stillbirth. Through this ministry, many women and their families have come to believe that nothing is impossible as God continues to work through his people.

Of course, Mary was the "first" Elizabeth minister. Off she went to the hill country to be with her relative in the last months of her pregnancy. We know from the mystery of the visitation what joy was shared by these two women, both pregnant, both bearing male children who would change the world. Nor should we romanticize this historical moment. Anxieties, fears, and doubts were part of the mix. Thus, to have one another was a great blessing for Elizabeth and Mary.

A number of Catholic hospitals have begun a new ritual. When a child is born in their facility, a soft lullaby is played over the speaker system. Nurses and other hospital personnel know immediately that new life has arrived. Whether Mary and Elizabeth could hear this background music is not known, but surely, in their hearts, a song was being sung. In fact, that song broke out into the open when Mary sang her *Magnificat*: "My soul proclaims the greatness of the Lord; / my spirit rejoices in God my savior. / For he has looked upon his handmaid's lowliness" (Luke 1:46-48a).

The Lord continues to do great things. New ministries emerge to address contemporary issues. New religious communities are established to do the work of contemplation and justice. Nothing is impossible for those who have faith in God.

Meditation: What are some of the great things God has done for you in your life? What are some of the great things you have done for God and others?

Prayer: Mary, on this feast of the Annunciation, we turn to you with reverence and awe. You found favor with God. You were called to be the one through whom the Savior of the world would be born. Help us to sing with you our *Magnificat*. Help us to serve others as you served Elizabeth and her child John.

Divine Hospitality

Readings: Mic 7:14-15, 18-20; Luke 15:1-3, 11-32

Scripture:
Tax collectors and sinners were drawing near to listen to
    Jesus,
  but the Pharisees and scribes began to complain, saying,
  "This man welcomes sinners and eats with them."
    (Luke 15:1-2)

Reflection: "Birds of a feather flock together," as the saying
goes. How strange, then, to see Jesus, the sinless one, eating
and speaking with sinners and others who were detested by
"respectful" citizens. Yet, that is exactly what Jesus did and
he made it very clear that the reason he came was to reconcile
everyone to the Father.

In his book *Preaching*, Fred Craddock tells the story of Carl
Sandburg, the poet and historian, who pondered what the
ugliest word in our lexicon is. Sandburg claimed that the
ugliest word in the entire dictionary was "exclusive." One
might argue with this judgment, but few would disagree that
exclusion is one of the most painful experiences of life.

Jesus' love and God's mercy are inclusive. It is available
to all, to the prodigal son and the elder brother, to tax collectors and prostitutes, to the rich and the poor, to the wise and
the foolish, to you and me. Like the sun that pours down its

rays on everyone without discrimination, so God's mercy is poured out on the entire human race. Those who are properly disposed embrace it; those who are ill-disposed fail to take in the grace.

The will of God is that no one be lost. Thus, Jesus came to seek out and save those who had drifted far away from God's mercy. And what joy when the prodigal son returns; what joy when the lost sheep is found; what joy when everyone realizes that they are welcome to God's table.

Divine hospitality was expressed well in a poem by George Herbert called "Love III." The first line reads, "Love bade me welcome." The poet goes on to speak of how the invited one begs off from entering God's (Love's) presence because of sin, because the invited one sees himself as unkind and ungrateful. But God, "quick-ey'd Love," pushes the issues and in the end the guest sits at the Lord's table and eats. Of course, each one of us is that invited guest and during this season of Lent we are given the opportunity of dining with God. Such is the inclusivity of God's love.

Meditation: What do you consider to be the most beautiful word in our language? Which is the ugliest? What weight do you assign to the word "welcome"?

Prayer: Lord Jesus, may we, sinners and saints, draw near to you and listen to your word. It is indeed the word of everlasting life. It is the word of salvation. Come, Lord Jesus, and bid us recline at your table.

Jacob's Well

Readings: Exod 17:3-7; Rom 5:1-2, 5-8; John 4:5-42 or 4:5-15, 19b-26, 39a, 40-42

Scripture:
Jesus came to a town of Samaria called Sychar,
   near the plot of land that Jacob had given to his son
      Joseph.
Jacob's well was there.
Jesus, tired from his journey, sat down there at the well.
It was about noon. (John 4:5-6)

Reflection: The well is a symbol of life. The formula is simple: no water, no life! Thus, everyone came to the well to sustain their physical life as well as the lives of their animals. But the well symbolizes more than physical well-being. The water at the well speaks of spiritual life, reminding us, from our Christian perspective, of baptism. We sense that Jesus is baptizing the Samaritan woman as he lovingly gazes at her and says, in essence, "You count."

The well is the site of conversation, a conversation that leads to conversion. Coming together at this source of life-giving water, Jesus and the Samaritan woman enter into dialogue. They are truly present to one another as they converse and banter and ponder about buckets, cisterns, and numerous husbands. The woman begins to move in another direction and has taken on a new identity. All this at the well, the site of dialogue and insight.

The well has yet another dimension: leisure. Jesus has been on a journey and is tired. The woman, too, probably had a busy morning and found life wearisome. Two tired pilgrims come together for a moment of respite. One senses that they truly enjoy each other's company though the disciples, upon returning from their lunch break, thought that this exchange was inappropriate. So much for human judgment upon the life of the Son of God.

Jacob's well is yet another answer to the question: "Is the Lord in our midst or not?" How can the answer be anything other than "the Lord is truly in our midst"—at the well, at the table, at our retiring and rising. The Israelites came to realize at Massah and Meribah that God's providential concern never fails.

Meditation: What do the well and water symbolize for you? Have you ever spent time in your imagination meeting and talking with Jesus at the well?

Prayer: Jesus, our life-giver, your love is inclusive. Everyone is welcome into your presence. You continue to come to us at the well of baptism, at the table of the Eucharist, on the dusty roads of human history. May we be attentive to your voice; may we experience the love and mercy in your compassionate heart.

March 28: Monday of the Third Week of Lent

Acceptance of God's World

Readings: 2 Kgs 5:1-15b; Luke 4:24-30

Scripture:
Jesus said to the people in the synagogue at Nazareth:
"Amen, I say to you,
  no prophet is accepted in his own native place."
  (Luke 4:24)

Reflection: In Fyodor Dostoevsky's *The Brothers Karamazov* we read: "Yet would you believe it, in the final results I don't accept this world of God's, and, although I know it exists, I don't accept it at all. It's not that I don't accept God, you must understand, it's the world created by Him I don't and cannot accept."

We have our vision of the way things ought to be. Doctors from out of town possess a certain mysterious wisdom; consulters from large cities surely know more than someone from our local agency; professors with a foreign accent certainly have insights that our native scholars lack. With such a perspective, we are ill-disposed to find truth, truth that is right in front of our nose.

Jesus, the very wisdom and power of God according to St. Paul (1 Cor 1:24), was not accepted in his home territory simply because he was from that locality. The locals must have asked how God's messenger could come from Nazareth. Surely, all great prophets must have other credentials, one of which must be an origin more prestigious than little old Nazareth in the foothills of Galilee.

Naaman, the leprous army commander, was offended when he was told to plunge into the Jordan, a river similar to the rivers of Damascus. Naaman was hesitant to accept the world as God had created it, to accept the direction of prophet Elisha. Nothing extraordinary here to merit one's approval. Well, Naaman took a chance and was cured.

Jesus was too ordinary for the residents of Nazareth. They knew his family of origin (or thought they knew it); they watched Jesus grow up; they knew the educational system of the village. So it should not be surprising that they refused to accept Jesus as God's prophet.

Do we accept the world as God has created it? Our task is to find truth in the whisper of God's prophetic messages, to find goodness in the cup of cold water, to find beauty in simple flowers and birds. And finding these graces, to respond to them by thanking and praising God and living according to his desires.

Meditation: Who are the prophets in your life? Have you rejected certain avenues of God's prophetic teachings?

Prayer: Come, Holy Spirit. Enlighten us to see and hear truth wherever it can be found: in local and foreign prophets, in ordinary and extraordinary events, in the quickening of our hearts.

Forgiveness: The Litmus Test

Readings: Dan 3:25, 34-43; Matt 18:21-35

Scripture:
Peter approached Jesus and asked him,
  "Lord, if my brother sins against me,
  how often must I forgive him?
As many as seven times?" (Matt 18:21)

Reflection: One of the most powerful stories of forgiveness unfolded in October 2006. A gunman, Charles Carl Roberts, entered a one-room Amish schoolhouse in Nickel Mines, Pennsylvania. He killed five girls, ages six through thirteen, and critically wounded five others before taking his own life. What shocked the country and the world was not only the killings but also the fact that the Amish community immediately offered forgiveness. Before the sun set on that fateful Monday, October 2, a member of the Amish community went to the parents of the killer and offered condolences. The Amish community also reached out to Marie and her three children, the family of Charles Roberts.

Here is grace in action. Jesus came to reconcile all creation back to the Father and that ministry of redemption has been entrusted to us. The basic message is that since God has forgiven us more than seventy-seven times, we are not to withhold forgiveness from one another.

Fr. Ronald Rolheiser, OMI, offers this reflection of forgiveness: "In a world and a culture that is full of wounds, anger, injustice, inequality, historical privilege, jealousy, resentment, bitterness, murder, and war, we must speak always and everywhere about forgiveness, reconciliation, and God's healing. Forgiveness lies at the center of Jesus' moral message. The litmus test for being a Christian is not whether one can say the creed and mean it, but whether one can forgive and love an enemy."

Peter pondered the question of forgiveness by asking how often that grace must be extended to others. Jesus again uses a parable to demonstrate that God's mercy is unlimited and that we, made in God's image and likeness, are to emulate that quality. It is quite obvious that, given the deep pain of being hurt, only by the grace of God can we do what the Amish community did.

Meditation: How often has God forgiven you? What do you understand by the Lord's imperative that we are to forgive "from the heart?"

Prayer: Lord Jesus, help us to be good instruments of your redemptive love. We find it so difficult to forgive; we find it so easy to harbor grudges and resentment. Send your Spirit into our world that we might cooperate with you to reestablish the unity you desire.

March 30: Wednesday of the Third Week of Lent

To Fulfill or Abolish: That Is the Question

Readings: Deut 4:1, 5-9; Matt 5:17-19

Scripture:
"Do not think that I have come to abolish the law or the
   prophets.
I have come not to abolish [them] but to fulfill [them]."
   (Matt 5:17)

Reflection: As disciples of the Lord, there are two questions
about Jesus that we do well to contemplate: who is he and
why has he come? The first question has to do with identity;
the second with mission or destiny. Peter proclaimed that
Jesus was the Messiah, the anointed of God. Today, Jesus
tells us of his mission: to fulfill the law and the prophets, not
to abolish them.

As disciples, what implication does this have for us?
Through our baptism, we are called to participate in the
ministry and mission of the Lord. We are called to do what
he did, to go where he went, to speak as he spoke. There is
no mission for the Christian other than the one Jesus shares
with us.

In his classic work *The Lord*, Romano Guardini beautifully
describes the mission of Jesus: "The young creature in the
stall of Bethlehem was a human being with a human brain
and limbs and heart and soul. And it was God. Its life was

to manifest the will of the Father; to proclaim the sacred tidings, to stir mankind with the power of God, to establish the Covenant, and shoulder the sin of the world, expiating it with love and leading mankind through the destruction of sacrifice and the victory of the Resurrection into the existence of grace."

In this "job description," we can feel the presence of God's law and the wisdom of the prophets. God's law is focused on obedience, doing the will of the divine Lawgiver, which is to keep the commandments that protect and nurture our relationship with God and with one another. The voice of the prophets is one that proclaims the good news of God's love and forgiveness; the prophets call us from sin and challenge us to be open to God's grace.

Jesus came that we might have life, and life in great abundance (John 10:10). His mission is all about fulfillment. The only thing that Jesus abolishes is sin and death.

Meditation: What is your mission in life? How does it relate to the mission of Jesus? In what ways do you promote fullness of life?

Prayer: Lord Jesus, renew the grace of baptism within us. You call us to be your disciples; you call us to follow in your way. May we fulfill the task your Father has given to us: to bring life and love to others. Abolish all sin from our hearts that we might be fitting instruments of your grace.

Division and Dissension

Readings: Jer 7:23-28; Luke 11:14-23

Scripture:
But he knew their thoughts and said to them,
   "Every kingdom divided against itself will be laid waste
   and house will fall against house." (Luke 11:17)

Reflection: Historians find it amazing that the American experiment succeeded. In the early days of the colonies, there was much division and dissension regarding taxation, slavery, forms of government, and so much more. The house almost fell. It was only through the leadership of such men as George Washington, John Adams, and Thomas Jefferson that unity was achieved, even though these political leaders had major disagreements.

Jesus knows the thoughts of the human mind and the emotions of the human heart. He is keenly aware of our demons and the forces of evil rampant in human history. He came to reconcile individuals and communities. Jesus came to free us from those impulses that alienate and separate us one from another.

The prophets were about the same ministry. Like Jesus, they knew the hardness of the human heart and the evil that can well up and destroy us. The prophets keep calling us to be faithful to God's voice, to walk in the way of the Lord, to do deeds of justice and peace. These messengers of God named our idols, our divisions and dissensions, our sins. More, the prophets instilled hope and presented alternative ways of being and doing.

Our responsorial refrain is a fitting mantra for the Lenten season: "If today you hear his voice, harden not your hearts" (Ps 95:7b-8a). Although Jesus knew the thoughts of the crowd, even more he knew their hearts. It is in this region of affectivity that the seeds of division and dissension abide. When Jesus drove out the devil from the mute man, in some way the mute man's heart was liberated. No longer was he enslaved by the power of deadly silence. Now, through the grace of God, the man was reconnected with his fellow pilgrims.

In his famous passage from the *Pensees*, Pascal writes: "The heart has reasons, which reason knows not, as we see in a thousand instances." Surely, the heart's deepest "reason" and desire is for intimacy, a oneness with God and others. Jesus came to foster that unity and peace.

Meditation: What is your personal history of division and dissension? How can we be better agents of unity and peace?

Prayer: Lord Jesus, you know the thoughts of our heart and the affections of our mind. You understand our human plight and the forces that divide and separate us. Come once again, Lord Jesus, and heal us of all violence and vengeance. Fill us with your peace.

More Questions

Readings: Hos 14:2-10; Mark 12:28-34

Scripture:
One of the scribes came to Jesus and asked him,
   "Which is the first of all the commandments?"
. . . And no one dared to ask him any more questions.
      (Mark 12: 28, 34b)

Reflection: Anyone even partially familiar with the New Testament knows both the first and the second of all the commandments: love of God and love of neighbor. Jesus' answer to the scribe's question was clear, definitive, and demanding. One wonders if the scribe had other questions to ask Jesus but hesitated out of either fear or not wanting to appear audacious.

But other questions, for that, do not remain silent. Questions such as: How are we to express our love for God, a God at once mysterious and incomprehensible, and how are we to love our neighbor when there is a history of alienation? Is love a gift to be received and transmitted or is it something that we do on our own? Are there limits to love, and is our tough love (disciplining, challenging, judging) valid or not? What is needed is a long lunch with Jesus to resolve these and many more questions.

Yet in today's passage, several things are clear about the nature of love. First, God is to have priority in our lives. Our

God of unlimited generosity has given us everything we have and are. We are in absolute indebtedness to our gracious, self-giving God. To the extent that we live in union with God, we will have the power to be in union with one another and all creation. It is when idolatry enters in, when someone or something other than God has priority, that our lives begin to disintegrate.

Second, our love for God is not to be partial or sporadic. The commandment contains the word "all"—all our heart, all our soul, all our mind, all our strength. Obviously, this does not preclude our loving others, as the second commandment states. Rather, in that total love of God, our sisters and brothers are included since God is Father of us all. To love the Father is to love his children.

Third, our love for others is to be expressed in a certain fashion—love them as we love ourselves. God desires that the active concern, reverence, and compassion we have received ourselves be given to everyone we meet. Such is the Christian life.

Meditation: What priority does God have in your life? What do you understand by the phrase "love yourself"?

Prayer: God of love and mercy, we know your commandments and your call that we share your affection and forgiveness with others. To do this we need the gift of your Holy Spirit; to do this, we need the presence of Jesus in our hearts. Grant us these graces, we pray.

April 2: Saturday of the Third Week of Lent

The Rest of Humanity

Readings: Hos 6:1-6; Luke 18:9-14

Scripture:
"O God, I thank you that I am not like the rest of
humanity—
greedy, dishonest, adulterous—or even like this tax
collector.
I fast twice a week,
and I pay tithes on my whole income." (Luke 18:11b-12)

Reflection: For anyone who thinks there is no humor in the gospel, all they have to do is listen to the prayer of the Pharisee just quoted. If a person has any funny bone at all, Jesus' parable is hilarious. The incongruity (the essence of humor) could not be greater. The Pharisee claims righteousness (after all, he does what we were asked to do on Ash Wednesday—pray, fast, give alms), but deep down he denies his membership in our muddy, messy humanity. More, the Pharisee doesn't just deny his humanity, he despises sinners.

Greedy! Avaricious are we all. Greed is one of the capital sins (along with pride, anger, lust, sloth, gluttony, envy). No one is exempt from having to struggle with these negative, destructive forces. The tax collector asked for mercy. He admitted his sin and through this humble confession went home justified by the grace of God.

Dishonest! Living in the truth is difficult. After the successful *The Road Less Traveled*, M. Scott Peck wrote *People of the Lie*. We so easily deceive ourselves; our disillusions are many. The "blind" Pharisee did not see the falsity of his claim that he was not like the rest of humanity. He left the temple, after his "fervent prayer," less free than he entered, for it is truth, and truth alone, that sets us free.

Adulterous! Everyone has to struggle with the fire and energy of human sexuality. It is built into human nature. Who is not tempted to misuse sexual longings? Apparently, the Pharisee. Denial here is especially dangerous because compensations will be found, be it in haughty self-righteousness, incredible arrogance, or even violence toward sexual sinners. We need but recall the woman caught in adultery (John 8:1-11). No one threw a stone that day, for no one was free from sin. Would that the Pharisee had heard the voice of Jesus and seen his face.

So, we are all part of humanity, struggling pilgrims, who stumble and often fall. It is the grace of humility that guides us on the road to truth and offers us some degree of freedom.

Meditation: Why is humility so critical to the spiritual life? Do you find humor in the parable?

Prayer: Merciful and loving Lord, guide us in the way of truth. Protect us from despising others or ourselves. Everyone struggles on this long pilgrimage. Grace us with humility and kindness (and a sense of humor).

Keeping the Sabbath

Readings: 1 Sam 16:1b, 6-7, 10-13a; Eph 5:8-14; John 9:1-41 or 9:1, 6-9, 13-17, 34-38

Scripture:
So some of the Pharisees said,
  "This man is not from God,
  because he does not keep the sabbath."
But others said,
  "How can a sinful man do such signs?"
And there was a division among them. (John 9:16)

Reflection: From God or not from God? We always keep coming back to the discernment question as we attempt to figure out if this relationship, this attitude, this behavior is rooted in grace or arises out of selfishness and sin. The issue at hand is the healing of the blind man, a good deed, indeed. But the miracle was performed on the Sabbath, that sacred day in which certain activities were prohibited. Of course, Jesus' vision transcends the limitations of any law, sacred or secular.

Lent is a season for discernment. Looking back at Ash Wednesday, the Lord called us to be people of prayer, people of discipline, and people of great generosity. How are we doing now that we are four weeks into Lent? Are we faithful in lifting up our minds and hearts to our ever-present God? Are we persevering in our "fasting" from food, from our selfish use of time, from our tendency to self-indulgence? And as for the call to give, are we not only just but sacrificial in sharing our limited resources with others? We are invited to discern whether our Lenten practices are from God or from some other source.

St. Paul, a master in the art of discernment, offers indications as to the presence of God's Spirit (Gal 5:22). Three signs stand out: love, joy, and peace. If our behavior, values, and relationships lead to an increase of these fruits of the Holy Spirit, we have some assurance that we are on the right track. By contrast, if chaos, sadness, and indifference characterize our lifestyle, serious questions have to be raised.

It is not unusual for people to be divided in the attempt to figure out what is of God and what is not. The Pharisees were divided because some of them gave great weight to the laws surrounding the Sabbath while others focused on the consequences of the deeds done on that holy day. Jesus kept the Sabbath by doing the Father's will: bringing life to others. We are invited to follow suit.

Meditation: How do you discern when an act is one of virtue or vice? How well do you keep the Sabbath? In what ways can the law foster life?

Prayer: Lord Jesus, help us to do what the Father asks. May we be respectful of laws that promote life; may we be courageous in doing the good, even if laws would make us hesitant. Heal our blindness and give us the grace to follow in your way.

The Whole Household

Readings: Isa 65:17-21; John 4:43-54

Scripture:
The father realized that just at that time Jesus had said to
    him,
    "Your son will live,"
and he and his whole household came to believe.
    (John 4:53)

Reflection: Ours is an age of individualism. Our thought patterns and our moral behavior tend to focus more on the individual, much less on the common good. Self-interest reigns; it's all about me; you've got to take care of number one!

Jesus was concerned about the individual and about the "whole household." In teaching the disciples how to pray, stress was put on "our" Father. We are all interconnected; we are all part of the same body, the body of Christ. St. Paul clarifies this by reminding us that when one person suffers, we all suffer, and, vice versa, when one person rejoices, joy comes to all.

The second sign that Jesus worked—the curing of the royal official's son—led to belief. But not only did the official come to faith, "his whole household came to believe." The same thing happened in the story of Zacchaeus (Luke 19:1-10) wherein salvation came not only to the tax collector but also to his whole family. The social nature of our spirituality has profound implications.

One implication is, as the Quaker Douglas V. Steere asserts, we have "unlimited liability for one another." A mature spirituality does not allow us to privatize our relationship with God. Although we do have a personal relationship with the Lord, there is always a corporate component to our religious life. The notion of being a pilgrim and traveling with other pilgrims illustrates this "unlimited liability" notion.

A second implication is that, because of our social nature, community has a high priority in the Christian life. We are church, a gathering of people in the household of God. We are called to share and care; we are called to compassion and empathy; we are called to respond together to God's will by acting justly, loving tenderly, and walking humbly in faith (Mic 6:8).

The royal official in Capernaum was in a life and death situation. His son was critically ill and the official begged Jesus to heal his boy. The official believed! And so did the rest of the family.

Meditation: What role do you assign to the social component of spirituality? How has the faith of others influenced your personal growth?

Prayer: Lord Jesus, give us the gift of faith. In our illness and struggles, we need your healing power. May our personal faith enrich the lives of others; may their faith in you help us to be better disciples. Come, Lord Jesus, come.

Well-Being and Responsibility

Readings: Ezek 47:1-9, 12; John 5:1-16

Scripture:
When Jesus saw him [the sick man] lying there
   and knew that he had been ill for a long time, he said to
   him,
   "Do you want to be well?" (John 5:6)

Reflection: Health is one of the most desired values in all of life. Well-being, be that of body, emotions, or our spiritual life, is a grace of supreme importance. Tremendous amounts of money, research, and energy are put into the healthcare field. As Emerson reminds us, "The first wealth is health."

Jesus raises a question in today's gospel that is directed not only to the man who had been ill for thirty-eight years but also to us: "Do you want to be well?" Do *we* want to be healed of whatever infirmity we have? Despite it being the Sabbath, Jesus cures the man on the spot, bidding him to pick up his mat and walk. But not only was the man cured of his physical ailment, the Lord makes reference to the man's spiritual life as well when he commands him not to sin anymore. The persecution directed at Jesus was as much at his spiritual healing as it was at his physical healing.

This wanting to be well has an interesting consequence. Once healed of whatever infirmity, we are now given new responsibilities and we cannot claim exemptions from ordinary tasks because of illness. So the thirty-eight-year-old ill man must now get a job and take on the duties of ordinary life. The person who is emotionally healed cannot continue to be excused from one's responsibility from solid relationships, hiding behind emotional distress. And the spiritually healed person, sins forgiven, must now take up those religious disciplines (prayer, fasting, almsgiving) that sustain spiritual health and help us to grow in the Spirit.

The philosopher Father William Lynch, SJ, reminds us: "With the ill, there is less relationship, less call, less response, more fear of help or response when it is there, and therefore far more trouble." It is no small wonder that some people do not want to get well, for good health imposes many demands on our life.

Meditation: What is the state of your health—physically, emotionally, spiritually? Have you ever hidden behind illness as a way of avoiding responsibility?

Prayer: Lord Jesus, you came to heal and restore us to health. May we have great faith in your power to make us whole. Through the gift of your Holy Spirit we can live full and productive lives, and even when ill, we can discern and do your will. We do want to be well and we praise you for the gift of health.

Nuts Falling from a Tree

Readings: Isa 49:8-15; John 5:17-30

Scripture:
"Amen, amen, I say to you, the Son cannot do anything on
    his own,
but only what he sees the Father doing;
for what he does, the Son will do also." (John 5:19)

Reflection: Principals and counselors appreciate the old adage about the nut not falling far from the tree. To understand a student's attitudes or behaviors, to understand a client's values and vision, the principal or counselor need but reflect upon the family of origin and in so doing come to a fairly good grasp of what is going on.

The intimate relationship within the Trinity of the Father, Son, and Holy Spirit is the concern of John's gospel. To understand the nature of our triune God, we must ponder the works that God does, and those works are creating, redeeming, and sanctifying. Jesus does what the Father and the Holy Spirit do, that is, give life and love to the world. That is why Jesus came, that we might have life to the full that comes to us through faith in the Lord and love for one another.

We are the children of God, God's beloved children. Hopefully we "nuts" do not fall far from the tree, the tree of life.

Made in the image and likeness of God, we are called to continue the works that Jesus and the Father and the Holy Spirit are doing. We are called to be agents of life, instruments of divine love, conduits of God's light.

But something has gone wrong. We tend to wander from the tree that has given us life. We tend to do works of darkness, not light; we struggle with self-absorption when we should be loving; we sometimes participate in the culture of death and fail in our mission of bringing life to others. Lent is the season to repent, to once again return to our baptismal commitment of being true disciples of Jesus. Like Jesus, we are to seek God's will and we are to participate in the marvelous works of God: creation, redemption, sanctification.

Meditation: What is God asking you to do? In what ways can you be an agent of God's creative, redeeming, and sanctifying love? Who are the people you have known who have done the works of the Lord?

Prayer: Lord Jesus, deepen our faith in you. May we hear your voice and follow in your way so that we might be agents of your Father's kingdom. May we live out our call to participate in your mission of salvation by being ambassadors of reconciliation. Come, Lord Jesus, come.

April 7: Thursday of the Fourth Week of Lent

A Burning and Shining Lamp

Readings: Exod 32:7-14; John 5:31-47

Scripture:
"He [John the Baptist] was a burning and shining lamp,
    and for a while you were content to rejoice in his light.
But I have testimony greater than John's." (John 5:35-36a)

Reflection: Ruth Mary Fox was on the faculty at the University of Wisconsin-Milwaukee for many years. She was a Dante expert and shared her wisdom of this literary giant in her book, *Dante Lights the Way.* Over the centuries, Dante has been a burning and shining lamp for readers who are seeking to understand the meaning of life. Dante gives testimony to one perspective of Christianity as he guides us on a tour down into hell, through purgatory, and up into heaven.

John the Baptist also points the way, the way to Jesus. This radical prophet knew his mission as being one of giving testimony to the Lamb of God, the one who would take away the sins of the world. But Jesus' testimony was even greater than John's as he gives us a tour of eternity, of the indwelling of the Spirit, of the great mystery of the incarnation and Trinity.

John realizes that Jesus himself was *the* light and that he, the son of Zachariah and Elizabeth, was a forerunner. He was to decrease as Jesus was to increase. But even here John was indeed a burning and shining lamp as he courageously took on Herod and preached a gospel of repentance. He was true to his mission and gave his life in his service to the kingdom.

Dante writes in *The Divine Comedy*: "Not many come in answer to this call." During this season of Lent we are once again given the call to holiness, the universal vocation of all people. John the Baptist answered this call by becoming a prophet; Jesus answered this call by embracing the Father's will; Dante said yes to the gift God gave to him. Our task is ultimately the same: to respond to God's call to live life to the full, even realizing that this only happens by dying to our self. When we participate in Jesus' paschal sacrifice, we become shining, burning lamps.

Meditation: In what ways are you a light (lamp) to others? How have you responded to God's unique call?

Prayer: Lord Jesus, guide us in your way. You call us to be salt and light to others. May we become shining lamps in a dark world; may we become a burning light that gives warmth to others. Draw us more deeply into your life.

Sent-ness

Readings: Wis 2:1a, 12-22; John 7:1-2, 10, 25-30

Scripture:
"Yet I did not come on my own,
   but the one who sent me, whom you do not know, is true.
I know him, because I am from him, and he sent me."
   (John 7:28b-29)

Reflection: In the postresurrection scene wherein Jesus asked Peter three times about his love for the Master, Peter testified that he truly did love him, and Jesus then explained to Peter the price of discipleship. To paraphrase: When young, Peter, you went around and did what you wanted and went where you willed. Now, however, as a disciple, you will be taken by the hand and carried off to places and situations that you would never have chosen (John 21:15-19).

Peter was invited into the life that Jesus lived: a life of being sent. Just as Christ was sent by the Father to reconcile all creation and bring salvation to all people, so the followers of Jesus, through baptism, confirmation, and the Eucharist, are sent on mission, often into places and situations that are strange, dangerous, and even abhorrent. No surprise then that in a culture of self-determination, the call to discipleship often goes unheeded.

What underlies this life of following Jesus is the need for discernment. What is it that we are being asked to do? To whom are we being sent and what is the message or type of presence that we are to bring? What are the signs that we are doing God's will and not our own? These and many other questions make the Christian life complex and sometimes very confusing.

To help us in the process of discerning our "sent-ness," we are given a variety of aids. For some individuals, spiritual direction is invaluable in sorting out what God is calling us to do or to be. For others, reading the lives of the saints is helpful as these dedicated souls exemplify lives of self-giving and sacrifice. For still others, keeping a journal and noting carefully God's proddings and nudges gets one in touch with the Sender. We are not alone in this call to mission.

Meditation: When was the first time you sensed yourself being sent on a special mission or call? How did you discern this being sent?

Prayer: Jesus, the Father sent you into our world to bring us the fullness of life. Help us to follow you as Peter did, being willing to go wherever you send us. May we not resist your call but may we, as Mary urges us, do whatever you tell us.

April 9: Saturday of the Fourth Week

The Greatest Speech Ever

Readings: Jer 11:18-20; John 7:40-53

Scripture:
So the guards went to the chief priests and Pharisees,
    who asked them, "Why did you not bring him?"
The guards answered, "Never before has anyone spoken
        like this man." (John 7:45-46)

Reflection: In *The Prelude*, William Wordsworth proclaims: "Oh wond'rous power of words, how sweet they are / According to the meaning which they bring!" The power of Jesus' words continues to ring down the centuries. Has anyone, have any of the great orators of history, spoken like him? Not only were people (even guards) taken by his presence and tone of voice, but even more by "the meaning which they bring!"

So what was the message of Jesus? Love your enemies! Here is a message that is truly revolutionary: it is not sufficient to reach out to those who are kind to us; we are to have deep concern and respect for those who persecute us. The message is backed by deed. Jesus, from the cross, forgave his murderers. Jesus looked across the night fire and forgave Peter. Jesus calls us to forgive seven times seventy-seven times. Who has ever spoken like this?

The message of Jesus is one of obedience. Doing the Father's will, being about his Father's business, reconciling all of creation back to the Father was his mission. That radical obedience challenges our propensity to get caught up in our own plans and designs. Christian obedience confronts our narcissism with the demand that we be for others. It is precisely dying to oneself, that grain of wheat falling to the ground, that brings new life. Who ever spoke so powerfully of life coming from death, of obedience leading to freedom, of sacrifice causing joy?

The ultimate message of Jesus was the sermon of the cross. In his *Poverty of Spirit*, Johannes B. Metz wrote, "And the legacy of his [Jesus'] total commitment to mankind, the proof of his fidelity to our poverty, is the cross." Over the past two thousand years, Christians kneeling beneath the cross experienced time and time again the power of *the* Word, this witness of God's love and mercy brimming with meaning.

Meditation: What has been the greatest speech you have ever heard? How does this oration compare to the sermon of the cross?

Prayer: Crucified Lord, help us to understand the meaning of your sacrifice. Open our ears to the message of your Father's love and mercy revealed in your crucifixion. Send your Spirit into our hearts that we may participate more fully in your paschal mystery.

Fellow-Feeling

Readings: Ezek 37:12-14; Rom 8:8-11; John 11:1-45 or 11:3-7, 17, 20-27, 33b-45

Scripture:
When Jesus saw her weeping and the Jews who had come
      with her weeping,
  he became perturbed and deeply troubled, and said,
  "Where have you laid him?"
They said to him, "Sir, come and see."
And Jesus wept. (John 11:33-35)

Reflection: The terms are many, the reality is the same. The terms? Compassion, empathy, sympathy, kindness, concern. The reality? Fellow-feeling. Jesus felt deeply the sorrow of Mary and Martha. The loss of their brother brought tears of sadness to their heart and anguish to their soul. The mystery of death overwhelmed them and the future held much ambiguity. Jesus felt the sorrow, the anguish, the ambiguity, and he wept along with them.

    Another occasion when Jesus wept arose again out of his compassion and empathy. Viewing the city of Jerusalem from a distance and realizing how many people were confused and lost, Jesus broke down and cried. Jesus knew that his mission was one of universal salvation. For anyone to be lost, much less a whole population, was just too much. These tears reveal to us the infinite compassion and concern of our loving, redeeming God.

What is at issue here is that radical sense of solidarity. We are one family; we are one people, all on the same journey back to the Father. What happens to one affects everybody. The great delusion is to think that we are autonomous creatures, self-reliant and able to go it alone. Nothing could be further from the truth. We come to God together or not at all. We have responsibility for our sisters and brothers.

"And Jesus wept." These are startling words and words that are to be taken with utmost seriousness. While our faith continually reminds us that Jesus is divine, that same faith tells of the humanity of Jesus. He experienced all that we do, except sin. Thus, we have a Lord and friend who knows what we are going through. Surely, Jesus wept for joy at Cana; surely, Jesus wept when Peter and Judas denied him; surely, Jesus wept, if only interiorly, when the adulterous woman was brought before him for stoning. Why else did he keep his head down while writing in the sand?

Meditation: Why is it important to keep our tear ducts open? What is the level of your fellow-feeling? What makes you weep? What makes you laugh, laugh with tears of joy?

Prayer: Lord Jesus, you know our inner pain at the loss of loved ones. Your tears at the death of Lazarus remind us of your tender compassion and rich empathy. Transform our minds and hearts to live deeply the reality of human solidarity. May no one stand alone. May we weep with those who weep; may we laugh with those who laugh.

The Art of Teaching

Readings: Dan 13:1-9, 15-17, 19-30, 33-62 or 13:41c-62; John 8:1-11

Scripture:
Then Jesus straightened up and said to her,
  "Woman, where are they?
Has no one condemned you?"
She replied, "No one, sir."
Then Jesus said, "Neither do I condemn you.
Go, and from now on do not sin any more." (John 8:10-11)

Reflection: There are different ways of teaching. Formal lectures inform the mind; seminars promote discussion and involvement; reading novels or watching movies are yet other ways of arriving at meaning and understanding. But perhaps the greatest teaching device is example. When we see compassion or love or justice right there before our eyes, lasting impressions shape our vision and attitudes and, ultimately, our actions.

  Jesus was teaching in the temple early in the morning. We do not have a record of what he said that morning, but we can be quite sure that it had something to do with his Father's love and mercy. Suddenly the session was interrupted. An adulterous woman was brought forward and the drama began. Here we find Jesus as the supreme teacher and the lesson taught was one of truth and compassion. The truth: sin is universal and thus the throwing of stones is prohibited. The compassion: no condemnation but the firm command to sin no more.

In one of his spiritual conferences, John Cassian notes: "The authority of a teacher will never be effective unless the fruit of deeds is impressed upon the heart of whoever is listening to him." So often in the gospel we see Jesus "doing" before "teaching." At the Last Supper, he washed the feet of the disciples and then asked if they understood what he had done. In today's gospel, Jesus again turns from formal teaching to teaching by action. Embedded forever on the heart of the woman and the accusing men was Jesus bending over and refusing to condemn. Herein is our salvation.

Is there any greater blessing than to have a good teacher who not only communicates truth but lives it? Jesus is our Teacher, indeed our Philosopher, who instructs us in the art of living and of dying.

Meditation: Who was the best teacher you have ever had? Did the teaching come more through words or example? To whom has God sent you to teach?

Prayer: Lord Jesus, draw us into the circle of your classroom. Be it early in the morning in a prayer corner or by taking us through the parables and stories of the gospel, instruct us in your way—the way of love and compassion and forgiveness. May we learn never to accuse; may we learn never to condemn. Give us hearts of mercy and love.

April 12: Tuesday of the Fifth Week of Lent

Belonging

Readings: Num 21:4-9; John 8:21-30

Scripture:
He [Jesus] said to them [the Pharisees], "You belong to
        what is below,
   I belong to what is above.
You belong to this world,
but I do not belong to this world." (John 8:23)

Reflection: One of the radical human tendencies is that of
belonging. We belong to the Boy Scouts or Daughters of the
American Revolution, to this or that political party, to this
parish or that temple, to the class of '98 or the Know-Nothing
Book Club. Except for hermits, and even they have their
annual convention, we are joiners and find total solitude
unbearable.

So, what about Jesus? What claimed his mind and his
heart? He tells us that he belongs "to what is above," to the
kingdom that his Father governs and guides. Paradoxically,
it is in "this"—namely, our—world wherein Jesus came to
do his ministry. Though he does not belong to it in the sense
that this world can claim his allegiance, nonetheless, Jesus
plunges into what is below to take it to what is above.

The Jesuit scientist and philosopher Teilhard de Chardin
maintained that all of creation will eventually rise and con-

verge. It is Jesus who is the one who draws all things back to the Father so that all creatures might find their true home. If we belong to anything other than God, we are restless and struggle with a sense of alienation. We are made for God; our true orientation is toward the Divine.

To belong to "this world" means that we have given ourselves over to power or pleasure, prestige or possessions. We wake up in the morning and realize that we are not free. We are possessed by our possessions. Jesus knows our human condition and he came to set us free. What gives us liberation is to live in the truth: the truth that we are God's beloved daughters and sons and our homeland is eternal life.

When the Israelites left Egypt and were wandering in the desert, they became impatient because food and water were in short supply. Understandably, they complained against both God and Moses and blamed them for their plight. The Israelites were in the center of one of those "belonging crises," those crossroads where we must decide to whom we belong. Those who opt for food and drink over freedom die; those who remain faithful and loyal to God's royal road live.

Meditation: To whom do you belong? What person, association, possession has a claim on your mind and heart?

Prayer: Lord Jesus, give us an appreciation for the things below, for the things above. Send your Spirit into our lives that we might make good choices. Help us to belong to you.

The "If-Then" Reality

Readings: Dan 3:14-20, 91-92, 95; John 8:31-42

Scripture:
Jesus said to those Jews who believed in him,
"If you remain in my word, you will truly be my disciples,
and you will know the truth, and the truth will set you
free." (John 8:31-32)

Reflection: Conditional clauses, those if-then constructions,
contain a fundamental law of the human condition. The
reality is that "if" you want a good harvest, "then" you must
sow and nurture good seeds. "If" you want to have good
health, "then" exercise and proper nutrition are part of the
ball game. "If" you want to stay out of jail, "then" abide by
the laws of the society.

In today's gospel we have one "if" and three "thens." If
we remain in God's word, then three things will happen: we
will be true disciples, we will know the truth, and that truth
will set us free. In a conditional situation, without the "if"
being lived, no "thens" will follow.

So how do we remain in God's word? Essentially, we do
so by living it! So when we read that St. Paul tells us that we
keep the whole law of Christ by bearing one another's bur-
dens (Gal 6:2), our task is to assist those whom God sends
into our lives, individuals and communities that are weighed

down by life's anxieties. When we ponder the last judgment scene of the separation of sheep and goats according to how the hungry, the naked, the homeless are treated (Matt 25), we remain in God's word by reaching out to those in need. St. John's great metaphor of the vine and the branches (John 15) drives home the point that only by staying connected to the source of life can we claim true discipleship.

The great "if" here can lead to two of the greatest gifts in life: knowledge and freedom. Truth comes from embracing God's vision of life. Freedom comes when, through a life of obedience, we do what we ought. Then there is another series of if-thens: if we know the truth and are set free, then we will experience deep peace and joy.

The philosopher Martin Heidegger maintained that the word is the "Dwelling-place of Being." God's great Word, Jesus, is where the disciple remains and in that friendship dwells truth and freedom.

Meditation: What words of God remain in your mind and heart? What influence do they have in your understanding of truth and your experience of freedom?

Prayer: Lord Jesus, may we remain in you and stay close to your words. We hunger for truth and freedom; we long for meaning and commitment. Open our minds and hearts to your vision and make us true disciples.

The Fragrance of Leaves

Readings: Gen 17:3-9; John 8:51-59

Scripture:
"Are you greater than our father Abraham, who died?
Or the prophets, who died?
Who do you make yourself out to be?" (John 8:53)

Reflection: Jesus made a promise that those who keep his word will not see death. Obviously, this demands a studied interpretation, for over the centuries both those who kept Christ's word and those who did not all died. This includes all the saints and all the villains of the world. Death is universal and there are no exemptions. So the question must be asked: what does Jesus mean by death?

Right off, we must exclude physical death. We all come to the grave, this being human nature. But Jesus is referring to eternal life and already, for those who are obedient to God's message, that new life is under way and physical death has no power over it. Abraham, the prophets, and all those who embraced the covenant and did God's will are alive and risen. They all share in the glory of God because of Christ's redemptive act.

So Jesus is greater than limited Abraham and all the prophets put together. Jesus is the manifestation of the Father; Jesus is our Savior, Redeemer, and Friend. He is the one through whom the sting of physical death has lost its power. As we approach Holy Week, we are invited to ponder and experience ever more deeply the redeeming grace of the paschal mystery.

It was John Henry Cardinal Newman (1801–90) who wrote, "We seem to live and die as leaves; but there is One who notes the fragrance of every one of them, and when their hour comes, places them between the pages of His great Book." We are not leaves of grass; we are "immortal diamonds" and are destined for everlasting life. Through grace, we do not judge by appearances but by the wisdom and the power of God, the person of Jesus, our risen and interceding Lord. It is he who existed before Abraham; it is he who established the new covenant, who is our hope and our salvation.

Meditation: How would you explain to a small child Jesus' words: "Whoever keeps my word will never taste death?" What do the falling leaves of autumn stir up in our soul?

Prayer: Risen and loving Lord, our finite minds and confused hearts are baffled by the mystery of death. Its finality seems overwhelming. Give us the faith to believe your words— words like, we shall never taste death if we believe in you— and to keep them in our heart.

April 15: Friday of the Fifth Week of Lent

God's Work and Ours

Readings: Jer 20:10-13; John 10:31-42

Scripture:
"If I do not perform my Father's works, do not believe me;
  but if I perform them, even if you do not believe me,
  believe the works, so that you may realize and understand
  that the Father is in me and I am in the Father."
  (John 10:37-38)

Readings: One of the great theologians of the twentieth century was the Dominican priest Yves Congar (1904–95). His three volume work, *I Believe in the Holy Spirit*, traces the history of the Catholic tradition regarding the teachings about the mystery of the Trinity and, in particular, the work of the Holy Spirit. Over and over again, Congar reminds us, in accord with the thought of St. Irenaeus, that the "two hands" of God are the Word and the Spirit. To Jesus is attributed the work of revelation and redemption; to the Holy Spirit is ascribed the mission of sanctification, inhabitation, and intimacy; and, to the Father, the work of creation.

What God does we are called to do as well, being made in the image and likeness of God. Thus, we are to be creative, that is, we are called to give life. This may sound obvious, but in a culture of death we realize there are many forces that block and even oppose the giving of life. War, abortion, euthanasia, and many other human activities violate the dignity of life. Jesus came to give life, life to the full (John 10:10).

Besides the call to be creative, we are baptized into Jesus' mission of healing and redemption. Jesus' vision is one of unity. Thus, each of us is called to be a unifier, fostering that wholeness and integration that is broken by sin and discord. This work that Jesus performed—in curing the ill, in raising the dead, in forgiving sin—is also the ministry of the church. It is through the community and its passion for justice and peace that Jesus continues to bring the kingdom of God into being.

The third work of the triune life is that of sanctification. Closely related to the mystery of creation and redemption is the call to grow and reach full Christian maturity. The indwelling of the Spirit enables and empowers individuals and the community to reach its full stature. We are not left to ourselves; God is with us every step of the way breathing life and hope and love into our lives.

Meditation: Which of the works of the Trinity do you find that you are called to do this Lent? In what sense do you do the works of Jesus?

Prayer: Loving and gracious Trinity, enlighten us to understand what we are to do. Make clear to us how we are to be creative, redemptive, and sanctifying on this pilgrim journey. May we find meaning and peace in emulating your work.

The Thickening Plot

Readings: Ezek 37:21-28; John 11:45-56

Scripture:
"What are we going to do?
This man is performing many signs.
If we leave him alone, all will believe in him,
    and the Romans will come
    and take away both our land and our nation."
    (John 11:47b-48)

Reflection: As we are on the cusp of Holy Week, we see the plot thickening. The chief priests and the scribes are planning to kill Jesus because he has become a threat to their power and their possessions, or so they suppose. As the crowds begin to believe in Jesus because of his marvelous deeds, the leaders become anguished and are puzzled as to what to do.

Caiaphas, the high priest, steps forward with a philosophical principle: better that one die than the nation be destroyed. Caiaphas was not concerned about the dignity of the individual but in numbers. His philosophy has emerged in every century since and "the one to die" has turned into millions. Jesus' philosophy was the exact opposite. Everyone is sacred and is deserving of our deepest respect.

Our gospel today is in the setting of the Passover. Just as Moses led his people toward the Promised Land, so too Jesus comes to lead people out of the slavery of sin and death and into the freedom of the children of God. Many came to believe in him and in his way of love, compassion, and forgiveness. Many came to realize that, in Jesus, the mystery of God was manifest in a new way.

We know the rest of the story. Jesus does die and his mission "to gather into one the dispersed children of God" will be realized. Jesus came to reconcile all creation back to the Father. And if this means suffering a violent death, so be it. The Father's will must be done; the people must be saved.

As Romano Guardini writes, "To be saved means to share in the life of Christ." It is here that we come to realize how much being a disciple of Jesus really involves. Not only do we journey with him in those glorious moments of feeding the hungry and healing the wounded, but we are companions of Jesus as he mounts the hill of Calvary. His dying is our death; his rising is our invitation to new life. Discipleship cannot be piecemeal, for it involves participating in all aspects of Jesus' life, death, and resurrection.

Meditation: Why did some people find Jesus so attractive while others found him so repulsive? What does salvation mean to you?

Prayer: Lord Jesus, help us to grasp the meaning of your mission. Empower us to participate in your gathering of all into one. May we be unifiers, fostering oneness where there is division, wholeness where there is fragmentation.

In Search of an Unshakable Faith

Readings: Matt 21:1-11; Isa 50:4-7; Phil 2:6-11;
Matt 26:14–27:66 or 27:11-54

Scripture:
Peter said to him in reply,
  "Though all may have their faith in you shaken,
  mine will never be."
Jesus said to him,
  "Amen, I say to you,
  this very night before the cock crows,
  you will deny me three times." (Matt 26:33-34)

Reflection: Flannery O'Connor, the Southern Catholic writer
of novels and short stories, claimed that all of her stories
were ultimately about the action of grace. It was faith that
drove the engine of her writing. She once made the observa-
tion that many people tend to think of faith as "a big electric
blanket" when, as a matter of fact, it is the cross. Our Catholic
faith is grounded in the mystery of the cross, God's revelation of divine love in Jesus' total self-giving.

  Peter felt that he possessed an unshakable faith. No matter
what happened, he would be loyal to Jesus. Peter had yet to
learn, as many still do, that faith is primarily the work of God
and not something that we do on our own. It is a gift and a
responsibility. It is a radical conviction about God's love and

a radical commitment to follow in God's way. There is nothing romantic about faith since it will demand of us what it demanded of Jesus: the laying down of our life for others.

Father Raymond Brown, SS, was of the same school as Flannery O'Connor: "All Christians believe through the prism of the cross." Faith takes us directly into the realm of suffering and death. Our belief holds that through the paschal mystery the world is redeemed. Our faith is a prism scattering the darkness of doubt and despair. In the end, it is being taken by the hand by a God who is the Lord of life and light.

During Holy Week we are invited to participate in the incredible richness of our liturgy. But there is more. As we celebrate in faith our divine worship, we are also aware that our faith must find expression in our social life, in our political decisions, in our cultural engagements, in our economic activities. Faith must be the engine that drives our entire lifestyle, one that is hopefully characterized by that of Jesus: a lifestyle that is simple, humble, and centered on doing the Father's will.

Meditation: What is the relationship between the cross and faith for you?

Prayer: Crucified Jesus, give us a strong and loyal faith. Like Peter, we are capable of abandoning you and your way. May we come to understand that it is your Spirit that empowers us to welcome you into our lives and to become instruments of your peace.

No Singular Sin

Readings: Isa 42:1-7; John 12:1-11

Scripture:
Then Judas the Iscariot, one of his disciples,
   and the one who would betray him, said,
   "Why was this oil not sold for three hundred days'
      wages
and given to the poor?" (John 12:4-5)

Reflection: Sin seldom comes singular. To cover up adultery, lies must be told; to perpetrate a fraud, deceptions must be employed; to escape a killing, disguises must be assumed. One sin breeds another and soon we are enmeshed in a bog of guilt and shame.

Poor Judas had three sins rolling around in his heart. The first, of course, was that of betrayal. Jesus chose him as a disciple and friend. They traveled together, they shared stories together, they ate at the same table time and time again. It wasn't as if Jesus was a stranger to Judas. Judas was handpicked and was destined to be an agent in the building of the kingdom. But then a deal emerged: for thirty pieces of silver, all he had to do was identify Jesus and kiss him in the garden.

Judas was a thief. Today we might call this some kind of addiction. But whatever the label, Judas stole from the common purse. Opponents of Jesus might have faulted the Lord for not doing an annual audit. They might have said that Jesus was naïve to trust this fellow with loose hands. All that put aside, Judas stole from the contributions given and was probably plagued by yet another sin, greed.

Add to this a third sin: hypocrisy. Upset that the costly perfumed oil had not been sold (Judas would probably be upset today that the artwork at the Vatican is kept rather than being sold to help the poor) and the proceeds given to the needy, an amount reaching that of three hundred days' wages, Judas feigned concern for others when, as a matter of fact, he was only concerned about adding funds to his own account. Betrayal, theft, and now hypocrisy—the list gets longer. One would hope that maybe Judas went looking around to receive general absolution.

In Khaled Hosseini's popular work *The Kite Runner* the character Baba states: "there is only one sin. And that is theft. Every other sin is a variation of theft." Theologians might argue with this but we know that theft leads to other moral transgressions, such as betrayal and hypocrisy. Judas is a case study.

Meditation: Do you agree that sin is seldom singular? From your experience, how has your sin led to other moral transgressions?

Prayer: Lord Jesus, have mercy on us for we have sinned. We have turned away from you and injured others and ourselves. Send your Spirit of forgiveness into our hearts; give us the courage to admit our sin and to return to you with contrite and humble hearts.

A Far, Far Better Thing

Readings: Isa 49:1-6; John 13:21-33, 36-38

Scripture:
Peter said to him,
   "Master, why can I not follow you now?
   I will lay down my life for you."
Jesus answered, "Will you lay down your life for me?
Amen, amen, I say to you, the cock will not crow
before you deny me three times." (John 13:37-38)

Reflection: Charles Dickens (1812–70), one of the greatest novelists of all time, had the ability to capture the human condition in all its rawness and beauty. In *A Tale of Two Cities*, a story that took place during the French Revolution (1789–99), we witness extreme brutality as well as extravagant human kindness. Like the events of this Holy Week, *A Tale of Two Cities* reveals betrayal and self-sacrifice, killings and redemption.

At the end of the novel, a law clerk by the name of Sydney Carton gives his life to save Charles Darnay, a husband and father. Although Sydney was not the noblest of characters, having his own sins and weaknesses, his sacrificial love at the end of the novel resembles what Jesus did for us: giving his life for another. As Sydney Carton approaches his execution by guillotine, we hear his interior monologue: "It is a far, far better thing that I do than I have ever done; it is a far better rest that I go to, than I have ever known."

Simon Peter was of the same mind as Sydney Carton. The disciple of the Lord was willing to lay down his life for Jesus if necessary. Peter was sincere. He loved Jesus and treasured their friendship. But we know the human condition and how, when fear overtakes the heart, we are all capable of cowardice. Every time we hear a cock crow, we might remember the times when we fled from our promises of self-sacrifice.

Judas was of a different temperament and moral character than Simon Peter. From the start, Judas was out for himself. Some form of greed dominated his personality and to feed that addiction he was willing to sell his master. The verse—"And it was night"—says it all. It was night in the depth of Judas's soul, a night for him that promised no dawn, although Jesus was himself the Light of the world.

Not only did Sydney Carton do "a far, far better thing" than he ever imagined, but he also came to experience that peace which is beyond all understanding, the peace of total self-giving. Peter would one day know that peace as well and we will too if we do that "far, far better thing."

Meditation: What is the greatest thing you have ever done in your life?

Prayer: Lord Jesus, give us courage to follow in your way, the way of self-donation. May we know that peace that comes from loving to the point of sacrifice; may we know the joy of participation in your paschal mystery.

April 20: Wednesday of Holy Week

Choose Life, Not Death

Readings: Isa 50:4-9a; Matt 26:14-25

Scripture:
"The Son of Man indeed goes, as it is written of him,
   but woe to that man by whom the Son of Man is betrayed.
It would be better for that man if he had never been born."
      (Matt 26:24)

Reflection: Back in 2009, Alexander Waugh wrote *The House of Wittgenstein: A Family at War*. The youngest son of Karl Wittgenstein, one of the wealthiest men in Austria at the turn of the twentieth century, was Ludwig, who went on to become a famous philosopher in England. Three of Ludwig's brothers committed suicide: Rudi and Hans in their early twenties and Kurt at the age of forty. One can almost hear in the background: better had they never been born.

But not so. Who knows the good that the brothers had done in their life? And who knows what brought about their despair and misery? What we do know, not of the Wittgenstein brothers, but of Judas, was that he handed over Jesus for thirty pieces of silver. The guilt and shame that came upon the soul of Judas was overwhelming and he took his own life. Better that he had never been born—what a tragedy all around.

All of this took place in the context of the Passover mystery, the liberation of the Israelites from their oppression in

Egypt. Just as the celebration of freedom was about to begin, we witness how freedom was misused. Judas betrayed his master; Peter denied his Lord; the other disciples scattered when Jesus was arrested. All this goes to prove that although we might think we are free and responsible, very soon we can turn the gift into a curse.

In the book of Deuteronomy, Moses proclaims: "I have set before you life and death, the blessing and the curse. Choose life, then, that you and your descendants may live" (Deut 30:19b). Jesus, the new Moses, sets before Judas, Peter, the Wittgensteins, and us, the same option: life or death. The choices we make shape not only our habits and character but also our very destiny.

The novelist John Cheever raises a haunting question that we might bring to prayer this Holy Week: "Oh why is it that life for some is an exquisite privilege, while others must pay for the seats at the play with a ransom of choleras, infections, and nightmares?"

Meditation: Why is it that some people choose life while others choose death? In what ways does Jesus call you to live life to the full?

Prayer: Lord Jesus, come to us in our weakness. Give us the strength to be faithful to you and your way of love, compassion, and forgiveness. Deepen our empathy for those who find life so burdensome; give us the grace to reach out to them in their discouragement and despair.

April 21: Holy Thursday

Towel and Basin People

Readings: Exod 12:1-8, 11-14; 1 Cor 11:23-26; John 13:1-15

Scripture:
So when he had washed their feet
  and put his garments back on and reclined at table again,
  he said to them, "Do you realize what I have done for
  you?" (John 13:12)

Reflection: Down through the ages there have been individuals who "realized" what Jesus did at the Last Supper. These towel and basin people followed the example of Jesus and washed the feet of those whom they met. These individuals, even though they too were teachers and "masters," focused on serving others, whatever their need. Who are some of these eucharistic towel and basin people?

One would have to be Blessed Teresa of Calcutta (1910–97), foundress of the Missionaries of Charity. Because of modern technology, millions upon millions of people witnessed Mother Teresa's dedication to the poor in Calcutta and around the globe. She insisted that her community need not do "great things" for God. Rather, it was in loving much and committing one's life to the poor that her sisters made an "offering of something beautiful for God." Jesus washing the feet of the disciples, in all its rich simplicity, offered something truly beautiful to God his Father.

A second towel and basin person was Oscar Arnulfo Romero (1917–80), archbishop and martyr of San Salvador. His country of El Salvador was torn apart by persecutions and violence. Archbishop Romero took on the government and the military, institutions that were killing the poor and blocking the work of justice. On March 24, 1980, while saying Mass at a Carmelite sisters' hospital, Romero was shot and killed. Like Jesus, he gave his life for others and became a voice for the voiceless.

Besides Mother Teresa and Archbishop Romero, another person who realized what Jesus did in the washing of feet was Dorothy Day (1897–1980), cofounder of the Catholic Worker Movement. This lay movement began in 1933 and her focus was not just on washing the feet of others, but on figuring out and doing something about how those feet got dirty. In other words, Dorothy Day sought to change the structures and institutions that deprived people of their basic rights. Her spirituality involved both doing the works of justice and living a life of charity.

Like the disciples at the Last Supper, it took some time before Mother Teresa, Oscar Romero, and Dorothy Day fully understood what discipleship was all about. But once they got it, there was no stopping them.

Meditation: Who are the towel and basin people in your life?

Prayer. Lord Jesus, give us the grace to serve others. May we emulate your example in reaching out to whomever is in need. Come, Lord Jesus, come.

Salvation: The Mystery of the Cross

Readings: Isa 52:13–53:12; Heb 4:14-16; 5:7-9; John 18:1–19:42

Scripture:
So they took Jesus, and, carrying the cross himself,
   he went out to what is called the Place of the Skull,
   in Hebrew, Golgotha.
There they crucified him, and with him two others,
   one on either side, with Jesus in the middle.
     (John 19:16b-18)

Reflection: Back in April of 2008, Pope Benedict XVI challenged the U.S. bishops to find new ways to communicate the meaning of salvation. He said: "It is becoming more and more difficult in our Western societies to speak in a meaningful way of salvation. Yet salvation—deliverance from the reality of evil and the gift of new life and freedom in Christ—is at the heart of the gospel. We need to discover new and engaging ways of proclaiming the message and awakening a thirst for the fulfillment which only Christ can bring."

On this Good Friday we witness our salvation as Jesus died for the sins of humanity. But the crucifixion, as a major symbol of salvation, has always been an event that defies comprehension. Even the great St. Paul struggled here as he preached nothing other than Christ crucified, which became a stumbling block for Jews and absurdity to the Greeks. Indeed, how can death lead to life? How can sins be forgiven through the mystery of the crucifixion?

Many individuals in Western culture see no need for "salvation." They claim to live respectable lives, not guilty of any heinous crime. They are good to their neighbor, do not steal or lie, refrain from greed and anger. So, what's the big deal?

The big deal is that fullness of life and freedom flow out of grace; the big deal is that the reality of evil is ever present, both outside us in our culture, and deep within us in our souls. God desires that all people be saved, that they are to be set free from every sort of evil and that they live up to their full potential through the bestowing of grace.

Would that we had a crystal ball to see how to proclaim the gospel in new and engaging ways; would that we knew how to awaken the deepest longings of the human heart. Even as we raise the challenge we feel our powerlessness, our need to be "saved" from futility and inept evangelization. Only through the guidance of the Holy Spirit will we do the work of the new evangelization.

Meditation: What is your understanding of salvation? Why is the crucifixion a stumbling block for so many, indeed, an absurdity?

Prayer: Christ crucified, give us the grace to understand more deeply the mystery of our salvation. Help us name the reality of evil within and around us; guide us into the new life of grace and freedom. Come, Lord Jesus, come.

April 23: Holy Saturday Night: Easter Vigil

Seeking the Risen Christ

Readings: Gen 1:1–2:2 or 1:1, 26-31a; Gen 22:1-18 or 22:1-2, 9a, 10-13, 15-18; Exod 14:15–15:1; Isa 54:5-14; Isa 55:1-11; Bar 3:9-15, 32–4:4; Ezek 36:16-17a, 18-28; Rom 6:3-11; Matt 28:1-10

Scripture:
Then the angel said to the women in reply,
"Do not be afraid!
I know that you are seeking Jesus the crucified.
He is not here, for he has been raised just as he said.
Come and see the place where he lay." (Matt 28:5-6)

Reflection: How can one not be amazed when a beloved who had died is no longer in the tomb? Mary Magdalene, Mary, and Salome were astounded to find the tomb empty. Since Jesus crucified was not there, they had to seek him elsewhere. Here is where the Easter mystery begins for us—our seeking of the risen Christ.

If we are alert, we will find our risen Lord in the richness of our sacramental life. Jesus is present in a supreme way in the Eucharist as he continues to give us his body and blood. Christ is with us as we anoint the sick, baptize and confirm our young and old, reconcile sinners to the Father, enter into marriage or holy orders. Through signs and actions we experience God's ongoing love, compassion, and mercy. In all the key moments of life—birth and death, love and commitment, and, yes, even sin—the risen Lord is present and manifest to accompany us on our perilous Christian journey.

If we are alert, we will find our risen Lord in the human community, both in its glory and in its misery. We encounter the risen Lord in the scholar who unveils truth, in the artist who expresses beauty, in the saint who incarnates the good. We encounter the risen Christ in the nursing home resident, in the prisoner on death row, in the stranger seeking a homeland. The gospel has great clarity in telling us that whatever we do to the least of God's children, we do to the Lord himself.

If we are alert, we will find the risen Lord in the great book we call the Bible. By prayerfully pondering God's word, we will encounter Jesus as the suffering servant, as the shepherd who never leaves his flock untended, as the teacher of great parables, as a friend and redeemer. We need but pick up the Scriptures each day to find Christ.

The tomb is empty. The Lord is not there. Rather, he keeps showing up in our sacraments, in the community, in his sacred word. Indeed, he shows up in the depth of our heart if we but listen.

Meditation: Where do you go to encounter the risen Lord?

Prayer: Jesus, crucified and risen Christ, deepen our faith in your presence among us. Help us to recognize you in the breaking of bread, in the cry of the poor, in the joys of human love. Come, Lord Jesus, come.

Easter Poetry and Song

Readings: Acts 10:34a, 37-43; Col 3:1-4 or 1 Cor 5:6b-8;
John 20:1-9 or Matt 28:1-10 or Luke 24:13-35

Scripture:
On the first day of the week,
   Mary of Magdala came to the tomb early in the morning,
   while it was still dark,
   and saw the stone removed from the tomb. (John 20:1)

Reflection: Sin and death! When all is said and done, we stand powerless before these devastating realities. Sin ruptures relationships and leaves behind a wake of guilt, shame, and broken lives. Death, that ubiquitous reaper, boggles the mind and has the appearance of such finality as to make human existence itself absurd.

It was into this human condition that Jesus came in the mystery of the incarnation. It was into this human condition that Jesus mounted the cross to redeem us from sin and broke the bonds of death through the mystery of the resurrection. In claiming to be the Resurrection and the Life, Jesus has set us free and has called us into a whole new existence.

Mary of Magdala, like all of us, had to deal with personal sin and the fact of death. When she came that day to the tomb and found it empty, we can only imagine what went through her mind, what she experienced in the depth of her heart.

She, like Simon Peter and John, would be tested in faith, but not for long, for all three eventually came to understand that Jesus had been raised from the dead.

In the Easter sequence we pray: "Christ indeed from death is risen, our new life obtaining. / Have mercy, victor King, ever reigning! / Amen. Alleluia." In this song of thankful praise we claim Christ as our redeeming Lamb, as the Prince of Life having conquered sin, as our hope and victorious King. When the mind falters in its understanding, we turn to poetry and song to express our faith. Only later can theology catch up and help our understanding.

This same poetry and song is found in our Easter preface: "We praise you with greater joy than ever on this Easter day when Christ became our paschal sacrifice. He is the true Lamb who took away the sins of the world. By dying he destroyed our death; by rising he restored our life." This is our faith; this is the faith of the church.

Meditation: How does the Easter feast affect your daily life? In praying the sequence and the preface for Easter, what do you experience in your heart?

Prayer: Risen and loving Lord, deepen our faith in your presence among us today. May we understand more fully your presence among and within us. In facing our sin and the mystery of death, give us the gift of faith and hope.

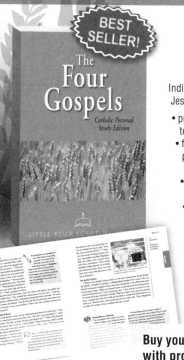